Wit At Several Weapons by Thomas Middleton & William Rowley

The play was originally attributed to John Fletcher & Francis Beaumont and printed in their early folios. However, though there is some minor work by Fletcher the play in modern times it has been now attributed to Middleton & Rowley. A version of the play re-written by Colly Cibber and titled 'Rival Fools' was produced but with no success.

Thomas Middleton was born in London in April 1580 and baptised on 18th April.

Middleton was aged only five when his father died. His mother remarried but this unfortunately fell apart into a fifteen year legal dispute regarding the inheritance due Thomas and his younger sister.

By the time he left Oxford, at the turn of the Century, Middleton had and published Microcynicon: Six Snarling Satirese which was denounced by the Archbishop of Canterbury and publicly burned.

In the early years of the 17th century, Middleton wrote topical pamphlets. One – Penniless Parliament of Threadbare Poets was reprinted several times and the subject of a parliamentary inquiry.

These early years writing plays continued to attract controversy. His writing partnership with Thomas Dekker brought him into conflict with Ben Jonson and George Chapman in the so-called War of the Theatres.

His finest work with Dekker was undoubtedly The Roaring Girl, a biography of the notorious Mary Frith.

In the 1610s, Middleton began another playwriting partnership, this time with the actor William Rowley, producing another slew of plays including Wit at Several Weapons and A Fair Quarrel.

The ever adaptable Middleton seemed at ease working with others or by himself. His solo writing credits include the comic masterpiece, A Chaste Maid in Cheapside, in 1613.

In 1620 he was officially appointed as chronologer of the City of London, a post he held until his death.

The 1620s saw the production of his and Rowley's tragedy, and continual favourite, The Changeling, and of several other tragicomedies.

However in 1624, he reached a peak of notoriety when his dramatic allegory A Game at Chess was staged by the King's Men. Though Middleton's approach was strongly patriotic, the Privy Council silenced the play after only nine performances at the Globe theatre, having received a complaint from the Spanish ambassador.

Middlwton for his part was exonerated but it is the last play recorded as having been written by Middleton.

Thomas Middleton died at his home at Newington Butts in Southwark in the summer of 1627, and was buried on July 4th, in St Mary's churchyard which today survives as a public park in Elephant and Castle.

William Rowley is thought to have been born around 1585 but an exact date is not known.

As an actor his early forte was playing 'clown characters' thus helping to carry the low comedy of the play. He began his career working for Queen Anne's Men at the Red Bull Theatre. In 1609. Along with several other actors he founded the Duke of York's Men, which, in 1612, became known as Prince Charles's Men.

From here on Rowley's career was spent almost exclusively writing and clowning for this company. It was located, in its time, at several playhouses, including the Curtain, the Hope, and the Red Bull.

Although when writing one of his main contributions was to provide the comic sub-plot on several other plays, including The Changeling, A Fair Quarrel, and The Maid in the Mill, he wrote substantial portions of the main narrative as well.

Only two surviving plays are generally accepted as solo works by Rowley: A Shoemaker, a Gentleman (circa 1607-9) and All's Lost by Lust (1619). Evidence exists that three other works were authored solely by Rowley: Hymen's Holidays or Cupid's Vagaries (1612), A Knave in Print (1613), and The Fool Without Book (also 1613) but unfortunately none have survived to be further examined.

In conjunction with other writers including Thomas Middleton and John fletcher he wrote several other plays.

The exact time and nature of his death is unknown but records show that William Rowley was buried on 11th February 1626 in the graveyard of St James's, Clerkenwell in London

Index of Contents

MEN

Sir Perfidious Oldcraft, an old Knight, a great admirer of Wit.

Witty-Pate Oldcraft, his Fathers own Son.

Sir Gregory Fopp, a witless Lord of Land.

Cunningame, a discreet Gen. Sir Gregories comrade and supplanter.

Sir Ruinous Gentry, a decayed Knight   } Two sharking

Priscian, a poor Scholar   } companions.

Pompey Doodle, a clown, Sir Gregories man, a piece of puff-paste, like his Master.

Mr. Credulous, Nephew to Sir Perfidious, a shallow-brain'd Scholar.

WOMEN

Niece to Sir Perfidious, a rich and witty Heir.

Lady Ruinous, Wife to Sir Ruinous.

Guardianess, to Sir Perfidious his Niece, an old doting Crone.

Mirabell, the Guardianesses Neece.

THE SCENE: London.

ACTUS PRIMUS

SCÆNA PRIMA

Enter **SIR PERIFIDIOUS OLDCRAFT** an old Knight, and **WITTY-PATE OLDCRAFT** his Son.

WITTY-PATE
Sir, I'm no boy, I'm deep in one and twenty,
The second years approaching.

SIR PERIFIDIOUS
A fine time
For a youth to live by his wits then I should think,
If e'er he mean to make account of any.

WITTY-PATE
Wits, Sir?

SIR PERIFIDIOUS
I Wits Sir, if it be so strange to thee,
I'm sorry I spent that time to get a Fool,
I might have imploy'd my pains a great deal better;

Thou knowst all that I have, I ha' got by my wits,
And yet to see how urgent thou art too;
It grieves me thou art so degenerate
To trouble me for means, I never offer'd it
My Parents from a School-boy, past nineteen once,
See what these times are grown to, before twenty
I rush'd into the world, which is indeed
Much like the Art of swiming, he that will attain to't
Must fall plump, and duck himself at first,
And that will make him hardy and advent'rous,
And not stand putting in one foot, and shiver,
And then draw t'other after, like a quake-buttock;
Well he may make a padler i'th' world,
From hand to mouth, but never a brave Swimmer,
Born up by th' chin, as I bore up my self,
With my strong industry that never fail'd me;
For he that lies born up with Patrimonies,
Looks like a long great Ass that swims with bladders,
Come but one prick of adverse fortune to him
He sinks, because he never try'd to swim
When Wit plaies with the billows that choak'd him.

WITTY-PATE
Why is it not a fashion for a Father, Sir,
Out of his yearly thousands to allow
His only Son, a competent brace of hundreds;
Or such a toy?

SIR PERIFIDIOUS
Yes, if he mean to spoil him,
Or mar his wits he may, but never I,
This is my humor, Sir, which you'll find constant;
I love Wit so well, because I liv'd by't,
That I'll give no man power out of my means to hurt it,
And that's a kind of gratitude to my raiser,
Which great ones oft forget; I admire much
This Ages dulness, when I scarce writ man,
The first degree that e'er I took in thriving,
I lay intelligencer close for wenching,
Could give this Lord or Knight a true Certificate
Of all the Maiden-heads extant, how many lay
'Mongst Chambermaids, how many 'mongst Exchange Wenches,
Though never many there I must confess
They have a trick to utter Ware so fast;
I knew which Lady had a mind to fall,
Which Gentlewoman new divorc'd, which Tradesman breaking,
The price of every sinner to a hair,
And where to raise each price; which were the Tearmers,

That would give Velvet Petticoats, Tissue Gowns,
Which Pieces, Angels, Suppers, and Half Crowns;
I knew how to match, and make my market.
Could give intelligence where the Pox lay leidger,
And then to see the Letchers shift a point,
'Twas sport and profit too; how they would shun
Their ador'd Mistriss chambers, and run fearfully,
Like Rats from burning houses, so brought I
My Clyentsa the game still safe together,
And noble gamesters lov'd me, and I felt it.
Give me a man that lives by his wits, say I,
And's never left a Groat, there's the true Gallant.
When I grew somewhat pursie, I grew then
In mens opinions too, and confidences,
They put things call'd Executorships upon me,
The charge of Orphans, little sensless creatures,
Whom in their Childhoods I bound forth to Felt-makers,
To make 'em lose, and work away their Gentry,
Disguise their tender natures with hard custom,
So wrought 'em out in time, there I rise ungently,
Nor do I fear to discourse this unto thee,
I'm arm'd at all points against treachery,
I hold my humor firm, if I can see thee thrive by
Thy wits while I live, I shall have the more courage
To trust thee with my Lands when I dye; if not,
The next best wit I can hear of, carries 'em:
For since in my time and knowledge, so many rich children
Of the City, conclude in beggery, I'de rather
Make a wise stranger my Executor, then a foolish
Son my Heir, and to have my Lands call'd after my
Wit, than after my name; and that's my nature.

WITTY-PATE
'Tis a strange harsh one, must I still shift then?
I come brave Cheats, once to my trade agen.
And I'll ply't harder now than e'er I did for't,
You'll part with nothing then, Sir?

SIR PERIFIDIOUS
Not a jot, Sir.

WITTY-PATE
If I should ask you blessing e'r I goe, Sir,
I think you would not give't me.

SIR PERIFIDIOUS
Let me but hear thou liv'st by thy wits once
Thou shalt have any thing, thou'rt none of mine else,

Then why should I take care for thee?

WITTY-PATE
'Thank your bounty.

[Exit.

SIR PERIFIDIOUS
So wealth love me, and long life, I beseech it,
As I do love the man that lives by his wits,
He comes so near my nature; I'm grown old now,
And even arriv'd at my last cheat I fear me,
But 'twill make shift to bury me, by day-light too,
And discharge all my Legacies, 'tis so wealthy,
And never trouble any Interest money:
I've yet a Neece to wed, over whose steps
I have plac'd a trusty watchful Guardianess,
For fear some poor Earl steal her, 't has been threat'ned,
To redeem mortgag'd Land, but he shall miss on't;
To prevent which, I have sought out a match for her,
Fop of Fop-Hall, he writes himself, I take it,
The antient'st Fop in England, with whom I've privately
Compounded for the third part of her portion.

[Enter **SIR GREGORY FOP** and **CUNNINGAME.**

And she seems pleas'd, so two parts rest with me,
He's come; Sir Gregory, welcome, what's he Sir?

SIR GREGORY
Young Cunningame, a Norfolk Gentleman,
One that has liv'd upon the Fops, my kindred,
Ever since my remembrance; he's a wit indeed,
And we all strive to have him, nay, 'tis certain
Some of our name has gone to Law for him;
Now 'tis my turn to keep him, and indeed
He's plaguy chargeable, as all your wits are,
But I will give him over when I list,
I ha' us'd wits so before.

SIR PERIFIDIOUS
I hope when y'are married Sir, you'll shake him off.

SIR GREGORY
Why what do you take me to be, old Fatheri'Law
that shall be, do you think I'll have any of the Wits hang
upon me, after I am married once? none of my kindred ever had
before me; but where's this Neece? is't a fashion in London,

to marry a woman and never see her?

SIR PERIFIDIOUS
Excuse the niceness, Sir, that care's your friend,
Perhaps had she been seen, you had never seen her;
There's many a spent thing call'd, and't like your honor,
That lies in wait for her, at first snap she's a Countess,
Drawn with six Mares through Fleetstreet, and a Coachman,
Sitting bare-headed to their Flanders buttocks,
This whets him on.

SIR GREGORY
Pray let's clap up the business, Sir,
I long to see her, are you sure you have her,
Is she not there already? Hark, oh hark.

SIR PERIFIDIOUS
How now, what's that Sir?

SIR GREGORY
Every Caroach goes by,
Goes ev'n to th' heart of me.

SIR PERIFIDIOUS
I'll have that doubt eas'd, Sir,
Instantly eas'd, Sir Gregory, and now I think on't
A toy comes i' my mind, seeing your friend there,
We'll have a little sport, give you but way to't,
And put a trick upon her, I love Wit pretiously,
You shall not be seen yet, we'll stale your friend first,
If't please but him to stand for the Anti-mask.

SIR GREGORY
Puh, he shall stand for any thing, why his supper
Lies i'my breeches here, I'll make him fast else.

SIR PERIFIDIOUS
Then come you forth more unexpectedly
The Mask it self, a thousand a year joynture,
The cloud, your friend will be then drawn away,
And only you the beauty of the Play.

SIR GREGORY
For Red and Black, I'll put down all your Fullers,
Let but your Neece bring White, and we have three colours.

[Exit **SIR GREGORY**.

SIR PERIFIDIOUS
I'm given to understand you are a Wit, Sir.

CUNNINGAME
I'm one that Fortune shews small favour to, Sir.

SIR PERIFIDIOUS
Why there you conclude it, whether you will or no, Sir;
To tell you truth, I'm taken with a Wit.

CUNNINGAME
Fowlers catch Woodcocks so, let not them know so much.

SIR PERIFIDIOUS
A pestilence mazard, a Duke Humphrey spark
Had rather lose his dinner than his jest,
I say I love a Wit the best of all things.

CUNNINGAME
Always except your self.

SIR PERIFIDIOUS
Has giv'n't me twice now.

[Enter **NIECE** and **GUARDIANESS**.

All with a breath, I thank him; but that I love a Wit
I should be heartily angry; cuds, my Neece,
You know the business with her.

CUNNINGAME
With a Woman?
'Tis ev'n the very same it was I'm sure
Five thousand years ago, no fool can miss it.

SIR PERIFIDIOUS
This is the Gentleman I promis'd Neece,
To present to your affection.

CUNNINGAME
'Ware that Arrow.

SIR PERIFIDIOUS
Deliver me the truth now of your liking.

CUNNINGAME
I'm spoil'd already, that such poor lean Game
Should be found out as I am.

SIR PERIFIDIOUS
Go set to her Sir—ha, ha, ha.

CUNNINGAME
How noble is this virtue in you, Lady,
Your eye may seem to commit a thousand slaughters
On your dull servants which truly tasted
Conclude all in comforts.

SIR PERIFIDIOUS
Puh.

NIECE
It rather shews what a true worth can make,
Such as yours is.

SIR PERIFIDIOUS
And that's not worth a groat,
How like you him Neece?

NIECE
It shall appear how well, Sir,
I humbly thank you for him.

SIR PERIFIDIOUS
Hah? ha, good gullery, he does it well i'faith,
Light, as if he meant to purchase Lip-land there:
Hold, hold, bear off I say, slid your part hangs too long.

CUNNINGAME
My joys are mockeries.

NIECE
Y'have both exprest a worthy care and love, Sir,
Had mine own eye been set at liberty,
To make a publick choice (believe my truth, Sir)
It could not ha' done better for my heart
Than your good providence has.

SIR PERIFIDIOUS
You will say so then,
Alas sweet Neece, all this is but the scabbard,
Now I draw forth the weapon.

NIECE
How?

SIR PERIFIDIOUS
Sir Gregory,
Approach thou lad of thousands.

[Enter **SIR GREGORY**.

SIR GREGORY
Who calls me?

NIECE
What motion's this, the Model of Ninivie?

SIR PERIFIDIOUS
Accost her daintily now, let me advise thee.

SIR GREGORY
I was advis'd to bestow dainty cost on you.

NIECE
You were ill advis'd, back, and take better counsel;
You may have good for an Angel, the least cost
You can bestow upon a woman, Sir
Trebles ten Counsellors Fees in Lady-ware,
Y'are over head and ears, e'r you be aware,
Faith keep a batchelor still, and go to Bowls, Sir,
Follow your Mistriss there, and prick and save, Sir;
For other Mistresses will make you a slave, Sir.

SIR GREGORY
So, so, I have my lerrepoop already.

SIR PERIFIDIOUS
Why how now Neece, this is the man I tell you.

NIECE
He, hang him, Sir, I know you do but mock,
This is the man you would say.

SIR PERIFIDIOUS
The Devil rides I think.

CUNNINGAME
I must use cunning here.

SIR PERIFIDIOUS
Make me not mad, use him with all respect,
This is the man I swear.

NIECE

Would you could perswade me to that;
Alass, you cannot go beyond me Uncle,
You carry a Jest well, I must confess,
For a man of your years, but—

SIR PERIFIDIOUS

I'm wrought beside my self.

CUNNINGAME

I never beheld comliness till this minute.

GUARDIANESS

 Oh good sweet Sir, pray offer not these words
To an old Gentlewoman.

NIECE

Sir.

CUNNINGAME

Away fifteen,
Here's Fifty one exceeds thee.

NIECE

What's the business?

CUNNINGAME

Give me these motherly creatures, come, ne'er smother it,
I know you are a teeming woman yet.

GUARDIANESS

Troth a young Gent. might do much I think, Sir.

CUNNINGAME

Go too then.

GUARDIANESS

And I should play my part, or I were ingrateful.

NIECE

Can you so soon neglect me!

CUNNINGAME

Hence I'm busie.

SIR PERIFIDIOUS

This cross point came in luckily, impudent baggage.
Hang from the Gentleman, art thou not asham'd

To be a Widows hind'rance?

CUNNINGAME
Are you angry, Sir?

SIR PERIFIDIOUS
You're welcome, pray court on, I shall desire
Your honest wise acquaintance; vex me not
After my care and pains to find a match for thee,
Lest I confine thy life to some out-chamber,
Where thou shalt waste the sweetness of thy youth,
Like a consuming Light in her own socket,
And not allow'd a male creature about thee;
A very Monky, thy necessity
Shall prize at a thousand pound, a Chimney sweeper
At Fifteen hundred.

NIECE
But are you serious, Uncle?

SIR PERIFIDIOUS
Serious.

NIECE
Pray let me look upon the Gentleman
With more heed; then I did but hum him over
In haste, good faith, as Lawyers Chancery sheets;
Beshrew my blood, a tollerable man,
Now I distinctly read him.

SIR GREGORY
Hum, hum, hum.

NIECE
Say he be black, he's of a very good pitch,
Well ankled, two good confident calves, they look
As if they would not shrink at the ninth child;
The redness i'th face, why that's in fashion,
Most of your high bloods have it, sign of greatness marry;
'Tis to be taken down too with May-butter,
I'll send to my Lady Spend-tail for her Medicine.

SIR GREGORY
Lum te dum, dum, dum, de dum.

NIECE
He's qualified too, believe me.

SIR GREGORY
Lum te dum, de dum, de dum.

NIECE
Where was my judgement?

SIR GREGORY
Lum te dum, dum, dum, te dum, te dum.

NIECE
Perfections cover'd mess.

SIR GREGORY
Lum te dum, te dum, te dum.

NIECE
It smoaks apparantly, pardon sweet Sir,
The error of my Sex.

SIR PERIFIDIOUS
Why, well said NIece,
Upon submission you must pardon her now, Sir.

SIR GREGORY
I'll do't by course, do you think I'm an ass, Knight?
Here's first my hand, now't goes to the Seal-Office.

SIR PERIFIDIOUS
Formally finisht, how goes this Suit forward?

CUNNINGAME
I'm taking measure of the Widows mind, Sir,
I hope to fit her heart.

GUARDIANESS
Who would have dreamt
Of a young morsel now? things come in minutes.

SIR GREGORY
Trust him not Widow, he's a younger brother,
He'll swear and lie; believe me he's worth nothing.

GUARDIANESS
He brings more content to a woman with that nothing,
Than he that brings his thousands without any thing,
We have presidents for that amongst great Ladies.

SIR PERIFIDIOUS

Come, come, no language now shall be in fashion,
But your Love-phrase, the bell to procreation.

[Exeunt.

[Enter **SIR RUINOUS GENTRY, WITTY-PATE** and **PRISCIAN**.

WITTY-PATE
Pox, there's nothing puts me besides my wits, but this fourth,
This last illiterate share, there's no conscience in't.

SIR RUINOUS
Sir, it has ever been so, where I have practis'd, and must be.
Still where I am, nor has it been undeserv'd at the years
End, and shuffle the Almanack together, vacations and
Term-times, one with another, though I say't, my wife is a
Woman of a good spirit, then it is no lay-share.

PRISCIAN
Faith for this five year, Ego possum probare, I have had
A hungry penurious share with 'em, and she has had as much
As I always.

WITTY-PATE
Present, or not present?

PRISCIAN
Residens aut non residens, per fidem.

WITTY-PATE
And what president's this for me? because your Hic & hac, Turpis and Qui mihi discipulus brains (that never got any thing but by accidence and uncertainty) did allow it, therefore I must, that have grounded conclusions of wit, hereditary rules from my Father to get by—

SIR RUINOUS
Sir, be compendious, either take or refuse, I will 'bate no token of my wives share, make even the last reckonings, and either so unite, or here divide company.

PRISCIAN
A good resolution, profecto, let every man beg his own way, and happy man be his dole.

WITTY-PATE
Well, here's your double share, and single brains Pol, oedipol, here's toward, a Castor ecastor for you, I will endure it a fortnight longer, but by these just five ends.—

PRISCIAN
Take heed, five's odd, put both hands together, or severally, they are all odd unjust ends.

WITTY-PATE

Medius fidius, hold your tongue, I depose you from half a share presently else, I will make you a participle, and decline you, now you understand me, be you a quiet Conjunction amongst the undeclined; you and your Latine ends shall go shift, Solus cum solo together else, and then if ever they get ends of Gold and Silver, enough to serve that Gerundine maw of yours, that without Do will end in Di and Dum instantly.

[Enter **SIR RUINOUS** and **SIR GREGORY**.

SIR RUINOUS

Enough, enough, here comes company, we lose five shares in wrangling about one.

WITTY-PATE

My Father, put on Priscian, he has Latine fragments too, but I fear him not, I'll case my face with a little more hair and relieve.

SIR PERIFIDIOUS

Tush Nephew (I'll call you so) for if there be
No other obstacles than those you speak of
They are but Powder-charges without pellets,
You may safely front 'em; and warrant your own danger.

SIR GREGORY

No other that I can perceive i'faith, Sir, for I put her to't, and felt her as far as I could, and the strongest repulse was, she said, she would have a little Soldier in me, that (if need were) should defend her reputation.

SIR PERIFIDIOUS

And surely, Sir, that is a principle
Amongst your principal Ladies, they require
Valour, either in a friend or a Husband.

SIR GREGORY

And I allow their requests i'faith, as well as any womans heart can desire, if I knew where to get valour, I would as willingly entertain it as any man that blows.

SIR PERIFIDIOUS

Breaths, breaths Sir, that's the sweeter phrase.

SIR GREGORY

Blows for a Soldier, i'faith Sir, and I'm in
Practise that way.

SIR PERIFIDIOUS

For a Soldier, I grant it.

SIR GREGORY

'Slid, I'll swallow some bullets, and good round ones too, but I'll have a little Soldier in me.

SIR RUINOUS
Will you on and beg, or steal and be hang'd.

SIR GREGORY
And some Scholar she would have me besides,
Tush, that shall be no bar, 'tis a quality in a
Gentleman, but of the least question.

PRISCIAN
Salvete Domini benignissimi, munificentissimi.

SIR PERIFIDIOUS
Salvete dicis ad nos? jubeo te salvere,
Nay, Sir, we have Latine, and other metall in us too.
Sir, you shall see me talk with this fellow now.

SIR GREGORY
I could find in my heart to talk with him too,
If I could understand him.

PRISCIAN
Charissimi, Doctissimique, Domini, ex abundantia.
Charitatis vestræ estote propitii in me jejunum
Miserum, pauperem, & omni consolatione exulem.

SIR PERIFIDIOUS
A pretty Scholar by my faith, Sir, but I'll to him agen.

SIR GREGORY
Does he beg or steal in this Language, can you tell Sir?
He may take away my good name from me, and I ne'er
The wiser.

SIR PERIFIDIOUS
He begs, he begs, Sir.

PRISCIAN
Ecce, ecce, in occulis lachrymarum flumen, in ore
Fames sitisq; ignis in vultu, pudor & impudentia,
In omni parte necessitas & indigentia.

SIR PERIFIDIOUS
Audi tu bonus socius, tu es Scholasticus, sic intelligo,
Ego faciam argumentum, mark now Sir, now I fetch
Him up.

SIR GREGORY

I have been fetcht up a hundred times for this,
Yet I could never learn half so much.

SIR PERIFIDIOUS
Audi, & responde, hoc est Argumentum, nomen est
Nomen, ergo, quod est tibi nomen? Responde nunc,
Responde argumentum meum. Have I not put him to't, Sir?

SIR GREGORY
Yes Sir, I think so.

WITTY-PATE
Step in, the rascal is put out of his pen'd Speech,
And he can go no farther.

SIR PERIFIDIOUS
Cur non respondes?

PRISCIAN
Oh Domine, tanta mea est miseria.

WITTY-PATE
So, he's almost in agen.

PRISCIAN
Ut nocte mecum pernoctat egestas, luce quotidie
Paupertas habitat.

SIR PERIFIDIOUS
Sed quod est tibi nomen: & quis dedit? Responde
Argumentum.

PRISCIAN
Hem, hem.

WITTY-PATE
He's dry he hems, on quickly.

SIR RUINOUS
Courteous Gentlemen, if the brow of a Military face may not be offensive to your generous eye-balls, let
his wounds speak better than his words, for some branch or small sprig of charity to be planted upon
this poor barren soil of a Soldier.

SIR PERIFIDIOUS
How now, what Arms and Arts both go a begging?

SIR RUINOUS

Such is the Post-progress of cold charity now a-days, who (for heat to her frigid Limbs) passes in so swift a motion, that two at the least had need be to stay her.

SIR GREGORY
Sir, lets reward um I pray you, and be gone. If any quarrel should arise amongst us, I am able to answer neither of them, his Iron and Steel tongue is as hard as the t'others Latine one.

SIR PERIFIDIOUS
Stay, stay Sir I will talk a little with him first,
Let me alone with both, I will try whether they
Live by their wits or no; for such a man I love,
And what? you both beg together then?

PRISCIAN
Conjunctis manibus, profecto, Domine.

SIR RUINOUS
With equal fortunes, equal distribution, there's not the breadth of a swords point uneven in our division.

SIR GREGORY
What two qualities are here cast away upon two poor fellows, if a man had um that could maintain um? what a double man were that, if these two fellows might be bought and sodden, and boil'd to a jelly, and eaten fasting every morning, I do not think but a man should find strange things in his stomach.

SIR PERIFIDIOUS
Come Sir, joyn your charity with mine, and we'll make up a couple of pence bewixt us.

SIR GREGORY
If a man could have a pennyworth for his penny, I would bestow more money with 'em.

WITTY-PATE
Save you Gentlemen, how now? what are you encount'red here? what fellows are these?

SIR PERIFIDIOUS
Faith Sir, here's Mars and Mercury, a pair of poor Planets it seems, that Jupiter has turn'd out to live by their wits, and we are e'en about a little spark of charity to kindle um a new fire.

WITTY-PATE
Stay, pray you stay Sir, you may abuse your charity, nay, make that goodness in you no better than a vice; so many deceivers walk in these shadows now a days; that certainly your bounties were better spilt than reserv'd to so lewd and vicious uses; which is he that professes the Soldier?

SIR RUINOUS
He that professes his own profession, Sir, and the dangerous life he hath led in it, this pair of half score years.

WITTY-PATE
In what services have you been, Sir?

SIR RUINOUS
The first that flesht me a Soldier, Sir, was that great battel at Alcazar in Barbary, where the noble English Stukely fell, and where that royal Portugal Sebastian ended his untimely days.

WITTY-PATE
Are you sure Sebastian died there?

SIR RUINOUS
Faith Sir, there was some other rumour hop't amongst us, that he, wounded, escap'd, and toucht on his Native shore agen, where finding his Countrey at home more distrest by the invasion of the Spaniard, than his loss abroad, forsook it, still supporting a miserable and unfortunate life, which (where he ended) is yet uncertain.

WITTY-PATE
By my faith Sir, he speaks the nearest fame of truth in this.

SIR RUINOUS
Since Sir, I serv'd in France, the Low Countreys, Lastly, at that memorable skirmish at Newport, where the forward and bold Scot there spent his life so freely, that from every single heart that there fell, came home from his resolution, a double honor to his Countrey.

WITTY-PATE
This should be no counterfeit, Sir.

SIR PERIFIDIOUS
I do not think he is, Sir.

WITTY-PATE
But Sir, me thinks you do not shew the marks of a Soldier, could you so freely scape, that you brought home no scarrs to be your chronicle?

SIR RUINOUS
Sir, I have wounds, and many, but in those parts where nature and humanity bids me shame to publish.

WITTY-PATE
A good Soldier cannot want those badges.

SIR GREGORY
Now am not I of your mind in that, for I hold him the best soldier that scapes best, alwaies at a Cock-fencing I give him the best that has the fewest knocks.

WITTY-PATE
Nay, I'll have a bout with your Scholar too,
To ask you why you should be poor (yet richly learn'd)
Were no question, at least, you can easily
Answer it; but whether you have learning enough,
To deserve to be poor or no (since poverty is

Commonly the meed of Learning) is yet to be tryed;
You have the Languages, I mean the chief,
As the Hebrew, Syriack, Greek, Latine, &c.

PRISCIAN
Aliquantulum, non totaliter, Domine.

SIR PERIFIDIOUS
The Latine I have sufficiently tried him in,
And I promise you Sir, he is very well grounded.

WITTY-PATE
I will prove him in some of the rest.
Tois miois fatherois iste Cock-scomboy?

PRISCIAN
Kay yonkeron nigitton oy fouleroi Asinisoy.

WITTY-PATE
Cheateron ton biton?

PRISCIAN
Tous pollous strikerous, Angelo to peeso.

WITTY-PATE
Certainly Sir, a very excellent Scholar in the Greek.

SIR PERIFIDIOUS
I do note a wondrous readiness in him.

SIR GREGORY
I do wonder how the Trojans could hold out ten years siege (as 'tis reported) against the Greeks, if
Achilles spoke but this tongue? I do not think but he might have shaken down the Walls in a seven-night,
and ne'er troubled the wooden horse.

WITTY-PATE
I will try him so far as I can in the Syriack.
Kircom bragmen, shag a dou ma dell mathou.

PRISCIAN
Hashagath rabgabosh shobos onoriadka.

WITTY-PATE
Colpack Rubasca, gnawerthem shig shag.

PRISCIAN
Napshamothem Ribshe bongomosh lashemech nagothi.

WITTY-PATE

Gentlemen I have done, any man that can, go farther, I confess my self at a Nonplus.

SIR GREGORY

Faith not I, Sir, I was at my farthest in my natural language, I was never double-tongu'd, I thank my hard fortune.

WITTY-PATE

Well Gentlemen, 'tis pity, (walk farther off a little my friends) I say, 'tis pity such fellows so endow'd, so qualified with the gifts of Nature and Arts, yet should have such a scarcity of fortune's benefits, we must blame our Ironhearted age for it.

SIR PERIFIDIOUS

'Tis pity indeed, and our pity shall speak a little, for 'em; Come Sir, here's my groat.

WITTY-PATE

A Groat Sir? oh fie, give nothing rather, 'twere better you rail'd on 'em for begging, and so quit your self, I am a poor Gentleman, that have but little but my wits to live on.

SIR PERIFIDIOUS

Troth and I love you the better, Sir.

WITTY-PATE

Yet I'll begin a better example than so, here fellows, there's between you, take Purse and all, and I would it were here heavier for your sakes, there's a pair of Angels to guide you to your lodgings, a poor Gentleman's good Will.

PRISCIAN

Gratias, maximas gratias, benignissime Domine.

SIR PERIFIDIOUS

This is an ill example for us, Sir, I would this bountiful Gentleman had not come this way to day.

SIR GREGORY

Pox, we must not shame our selves now, Sir, I'll give as much as that Gentleman, though I never be Soldier or Scholar while I live; here friends, there's a piece, that if he were divided, would make a pair of Angels for me too, in the love I bear to the Sword and the Tongues.

SIR PERIFIDIOUS

My largess shall be equal too, and much good do you, this bounty is a little abatement of my wit, though I feel that.

SIR RUINOUS

May soldiers ever defend such charities.

PRISCIAN

And Scholars pray for their increase.

SIR PERIFIDIOUS

Fare you well, Sir, these fellows may pray for you, you have made the Scholars Commons exceed to day, and a word with you, Sir, you said you liv'd by your wits, if you use this bounty, you'll begger your wits, believe it.

WITTY-PATE

Oh Sir, I hope to encrease 'em by it, this seed never wants his harvest, fare you well, Sir.

[Exit.

SIR GREGORY

I think a man were as good meet with a reasonable Thief, as an unreasonable Begger sometimes, I could find in my heart to beg half mine back agen, can you change my piece my friends?

PRISCIAN

Tempora mutantur, & nos mutamur in illis.

SIR GREGORY

My Gold is turn'd into Latine.

[Enter **WITTY-PATE**.

Look you good fellows, here's one round
Shilling more that lay conceal'd.

SIR PERIFIDIOUS

Sir, away, we shall be drawn farther into damage else.

SIR GREGORY

A pox of the Fool, he live by his wits? if his wits leave him any money, but what he begs or steals very shortly, I'll be hang'd for him.

[Exeunt the **TWO KNIGHTS**.

SIR RUINOUS

This breakfast parcel was well fetcht off i'faith.

WITTY-PATE

Tush, a by-blow for mirth, we must have better purchase, we want a fourth for another project that I have ripen'd.

SIR RUINOUS

My wife she shares, and can deserve it.

WITTY-PATE

She can change her shape, and be masculine.

SIR RUINOUS

'Tis one of the free'st conditions, she fears not the crack of a Pistol, she dares say Stand to a Grazier.

PRISCIAN
Probatum fuit, profecto Domine.

WITTY-PATE
Good, then you Sir Bacchus, Apollo shall be dispatcht with her share, and some contents to meet us to morrow (at a certain place and time appointed) in the Masculine Gender, my Father has a Nephew, and I an own Cosin coming up from the University, whom he loves most indulgently, easie Master Credulous Oldcraft, (for you know what your meer Academique is) your Carrier never misses his hour, he must not be rob'd (because he has but little to lose) but he must joyn with us in a devise that I have, that shall rob my Father of a hundred pieces, and thank me to be rid on't, for there's the ambition of my wit, to live upon his profest wit, that has turn'd me out to live by my wits.

PRISCIAN
Cum hirundinis alis tibi regratulor.

WITTY-PATE
A male habit, a bag of an hunder'd weight, though it be Counters (for my Alchimy shall turn 'em into Gold of my Fathers) the hour, the place, the action shall be at large set down, and Father, you shall know, that I put my portion to use, that you have given me to live by;

And to confirm your self in me renate,
I hope you'll find my wits legitimate.

[Exeunt.

ACTUS SECUNDUS

SCÆNA PRIMA

Enter **LADY** and **SERVANTS**.

SERVANT
Nay Lady.

LADY
Put me not in mind on't, prethee,
You cannot do a greater wrong to Women,
For in our wants, 'tis the most chief affliction
To have that name remembred; 'tis a Title
That misery mocks us by, and the worlds malice,
Scorn and contempt has not wherewith to work
On humble Callings; they are safe, and lye
Level with pitty still, and pale distress
Is no great stranger to 'em; but when fortune

Looks with a stormy face on our conditions,
We find affliction work, and envy pastime,
And our worst enemy than that most abuses us,
Is that we are call'd by, Lady, Oh my spirit,
Will nothing make thee humble? I am well methinks,
And can live quiet with my fate sometimes,
Until I look into the world agen,
Then I begin to rave at my Stars bitterness,
To see how many muckhils plac'd above me;
Peasants and Droyls, Caroches full of Dunghils,
Whose very birth stinks in a generous nostril,
Glistring by night like Glow-worms through the High streets
Hurried by Torch-light in the Foot-mans hands
That shew like running Fire-drakes through the City,
And I put to my shifts and wits to live,
Nay sometimes danger too; on Foot, on Horseback,
And earn my supper manfully e'r I get it,
Many a meal I have purchas'd at that rate,

[Enter **PRISCIAN**.

Fed with a wound upon me, stampt at midnight.
Hah, what are you?

PRISCIAN
Now you may tell your self, Lady.

[Pulls off's beard.

LADY
Oh Mr. Priscian, what's the project,
For you n'er come without one.

PRISCIAN
First, your Husband,
Sir Ruinous Gentry greets you with best wishes,
And here has sent you your full share by me
In five Cheats and two Robberies.

LADY
And what comes it too?

PRISCIAN
Near upon thirteen pound.

LADY
A goodly share,
'Twill put a Lady scarce in Philip and Cheyney,

With three small Bugle Laces, like a Chambermaid,
Here's precious lifting.

PRISCIAN
'Las you must consider, Lady,
'Tis but young Term, Attornies ha small doings yet,
Then Highway Lawyers, they must needs ha little,
We'ave had no great good luck to speak troth, Beauty,
Since your stout Ladyship parted from's at Highgate,
But there's a fair hope now for a present hunder'd,
Here's mans Apparel, your Horse stands at door.

LADY
And what's the virtuous plot now?

PRISCIAN
Marry Lady,
You, like a brave young Gallant must be robb'd.

LADY
I robb'd?

PRISCIAN
Nay then—

LADY
Well, well, go on, let's hear Sir.

PRISCIAN
Here's a seal'd bag of a Hunder'd, which indeed
Are Counters all, only some sixteen Groats
Of white money i'th' mouth on't.

LADY
So, what Saddle have I?

PRISCIAN
Monsieur Laroon's the Frenchmans.

LADY
That agen,
You know so well it is not for my stride,
How oft have I complain'd on't?

PRISCIAN
You may have Jockey's then, the little Scotch one,
You must dispatch.

[Exit **PRISCIAN**.

LADY
I'll soon be ready, Sir,
Before you ha shifted Saddles, many Women
Have their wealth flow to 'em, I was made I see
To help my fortune, not my fortune me.

[Exit.

[Enter **CUNNINGAME**.

CUNNINGAME
My ways are Goblin-led, and the night-Elf
Still draws me from my home, yet I follow,
Sure, 'tis not altogether fabulous,
Such Haggs do get dominion of our tongues
So soon as we speak, the Inchantment binds;
I have dissembled such a trouble on me,
As my best wits can hardly clear agen;
Piping through this old reed, the Guardianess,
With purpose that my harmony shall reach
And please the Ladies ear, she stops below,
And ecchoes back my Love unto my Lips,
Perswaded by most violent arguments
Of self-love in her self; I am so self-fool,
To doat upon her hunder'd wrinkl'd face;
I could beggar her to accept the gifts
She would throw upon me; 'twere charity,
But for pities sake I will be a niggard
And undo her, refusing to take from her;
I'm haunted agen, if it take not now
I'll break the Spell.

[Enter **GUARDIANESS**.

GUARDIANESS
Sweet Cunningame, welcome;
What? a whole day absent? Birds that build Nests
Have care to keep 'em.

CUNNINGAME
That's granted,
But not continually to sit upon 'em;
Less in the youngling season, else they desire
To fly abroad, and recreate their labours,
Then they return with fresher appetite
To work agen.

GUARDIANESS
Well, well, you have built a Nest
That will stand all storms, you need not mistrust
A weather-wrack, and one day it may be
The youngling season too, then I hope
You'll ne'er fly out of sight.

CUNNINGAME
There will be pains,
I see to shake this Burr off, and sweetest,
Prethee how fares thy charge? has my good friend
Sir Gregory, the countenance of a Lover?

GUARDIANESS
No by my troth, not in my mind, methinks
(Setting his Worship aside) he looks like a fool.

CUNNINGAME
Nay i'faith, ne'r divide his Worship from him for that
Small matter; Fool and Worship are no such
Strangers now adaies, but my meaning is,
Has he thy Ladies countenance of Love?
Looks she like a welcome on him? plainly,
Have they as good hope of one another,
As Cupid bless us, we have?

GUARDIANESS
Troth I know not,
I can perceive no forwardness in my charge,
But I protest I wish the Knight better
For your sake, Bird.

CUNNINGAME
Why thanks sweet Bird, and with my heart I wish,
That he had as strong and likely hope of her
As thou hast of me.

GUARDIANESS
Well, he's like to speed
Ne'er the worse for that good wish, and I'll tell you
Bird (for secrets are not to be kept betwixt us two)
My charge thinks well of you.

CUNNINGAME
Of me? for what?

GUARDIANESS

For my sake, I mean so, I have heard her
A hundred times, since her Uncle gave her
The first bob about you, that she'd doe somewhat
For my sake, if things went well together,
We have spoke of doors and bolts, and things and things,
Go too, I'll tell you all, but you'll find
Some advancement, for my sake, I do believe.

CUNNINGAME
Faith be not sparing, tell me.

GUARDIANESS
By my Lady
You shall pardon me for that, 'twere a shame
If men should hear all that women speak behind
Their backs sometimes.

CUNNINGAME
You must give me leave yet,
At least to give her thanks.

GUARDIANESS
Nor that neither,
She must not take a notice of my blabbing,
It is sufficient you shall give me thanks,
For 'tis for my sake if she be bountiful,
She loves me, and loves you too for my sake.

CUNNINGAME
How shall I, knowing this, but be ingrate,
Not to repay her with my dearest duty.

GUARDIANESS
I, but you must not know it, if you tell
All that I open to you; you'll shame us both;
A far off you may kiss your hand, blush or so,
But I'll allow no nearer conference.

CUNNINGAME
Whoop! you'll be jealous I perceive now.

GUARDIANESS
Jealous? why there's no true love without it, Bird,
I must be jealous of thee, but for her,
(Were it within my duty to my Master)
I durst trust her with the strongest tempter,
And I dare swear her now as pure a Virgin
As e'er was welcom'd to a marriage bed;

If thoughts may be untainted, hers are so.

CUNNINGAME
And where's the cause of your fear then?

GUARDIANESS
Well, well;
When things are past, and the wedding Torches
Lighted at Matches, to kindle better fire,
Then I'll tell you more.

CUNNINGAME
Come, come, I see farther,
That if we were married, you'd be jealous.

GUARDIANESS
I protest I should a little, but not of her
It is the married woman (if you mark it)
And not the Maid that longs, the appetite
Follows the first taste, when we have relisht
We wish cloying, the taste once pleas'd before,
Then our desire is whetted on to more,
But I reveal too much to you, i'faith Bird.

CUNNINGAME
Not a whit i'faith, Bird, betwixt you and I,
I am beholding for bettering of my knowledg.

GUARDIANESS
Nay, you shall know more of me, if you'll be rul'd
But make not things common.

CUNNINGAME
Ud' so, your Lady?

GUARDIANESS
I, 'tis no matter, she'll like well of this,
Our familiarity is her content.

[Enter **NIECE** and **CLOWN**.

NIECE
This present from Sir Gregory?

CLOWN
From my Master, the Worshipful, right Sir Gregory Fop.

NIECE

A Ruffe? and what might be his high conceit
In sending of a Ruff?

CLOWN
I think he had two conceits in it forsooth, too high too Low, Ruff high, because as the Ruff does embrace your neck all day, so does he desire to throw his Knightly Arms.

NIECE
But then I leave him off a-nights.

CLOWN
Why then he is ruffe low, a ruffian, a bold adventurous errand to do any rough service for his Lady.

NIECE [Toward **CUNNINGAME**]
A witty and unhappy conceit, does he mean
As he seems to say unto that reverence?
He does wooe her sure.

CLOWN
To tell you truth, Lady, his conceit was far better than I have blaz'd it yet.

NIECE
Do you think so, Sir?

CLOWN
Nay, I know it forsooth, for it was two days, e'r he compass'd it, to find a fitting present for your Ladyship, he was sending once a very fine Puppy to you.

NIECE
And that he would have brought himself.

CLOWN
So he would indeed, but then he alter'd his device, and sent this Ruffe; requesting withall, that whensoever it is foul, you (with your own hands) would bestow the starching of it.

NIECE [Toward **CUNNINGAME**]
Else she wooes him, now his eyes shoots this way;
And what was the reason for that, Sir?

CLOWN
There lies his main conceit, Lady, for says he, In so doing she cannot chuse but in the starching, to clap it often between her hands, and so she gives a great liking and applause to my Present, whereas, if I should send a Puppy, she ever calls it to her with hist, hiss, hiss, which is a fearful disgrace, he drew the device from a Play, at the Bull tother day.

NIECE
I marry Sir, this was a rich conceit indeed.

CLOWN
And far fetch'd, therefore good for you, Lady.

GUARDIANESS
How now? which way look you, Bird?

CUNNINGAME
At the Fool Bird, shall I not look at the Fool?

GUARDIANESS
At the Fool and I here? what need that? pray look this way.

NIECE
I'll fit him aptly, either I'll awake
His wits (if he have any,) or force him
To appear (as yet I cannot think him)
Without any. Sirrah, tell me one thing true
That I shall aske you now, Was this device
Your Masters own? I doubt his wit in it;
He's not so ingenius.

CLOWN
His own I assure you, Madam.

NIECE
Nay, you must not lye.

CLOWN
Not with a Lady, I'd rather lye with you, than lie with my Master, by your leave in such a case as this.

GUARDIANESS
Yet agen your eye?

CUNNINGAME
The fool makes mirth i'faith,
I would hear some.

GUARDIANESS
Come, you shall hear none but me.

NIECE
Come hither, friend, nay, come nearer me; did
Thy Master send thee to me? he may be wise,
But did not shew it much in that; men sometimes
May wrong themselves unawares, when they least think on't;
Was Vulcan ever so unwise to send Mars
To be his spokesman, when he went a wooing?
Send thee? hey-ho, a pretty rowling eye.

CLOWN

I can turn up the white and the black too, and need be forsooth.

NIECE

Why, here's an amorous nose.

CLOWN

You see the worst of my nose, forsooth.

NIECE

A cheek, how I could put it now in dalliance,
A pair of Lips, oh that we were uney'd,
I could suck Sugar from 'em, what a beard's here!
When will the Knight thy Master have such a
Stamp of manhood on his face? nay, do not blush.

CLOWN

'Tis nothing but my flesh and blood that rises so.

CUNNINGAME

'Death, she courts the fool.

GUARDIANESS

Away, away, 'tis sport, do not mind it.

NIECE

Give me thy hand, come, be familiar;
I, here's a promising palm; what a soft
Handful of pleasure's here, here's Down compar'd
With Flocks and quilted Straw, thy Knights fingers
Are lean mattrice rubbers to these Feathers,
I prethee let me lean my cheek upon't.
What a soft pillow's here!

CLOWN

Hum, umh, hu, hum.

NIECE

Why there's a courage in that lively passion,
Measure thee all o'r, there's not a limb
But has his full proportion, it is my voice,
There's no compare betwixt the Knight and thee,
The goodlier man by half, at once now
I see thee all over.

CLOWN

If you had seen me swim t'other day on my back, you would have sed you had seen, there was two Chambermaids that saw me, and my legs by chance were tangled in the flags, and when they saw how I was hang'd, they cryed out, Oh help the man for fear he be drown'd.

NIECE
They could do no less in pity, come thine arm, we'll walk together.

CUNNINGAME
Blindness of Love and Women, why she dotes upon the fool.

GUARDIANESS
What's that to you, mind her not.

CUNNINGAME
Away you Burr.

GUARDIANESS
How's that?

CUNNINGAME
Hang of Fleshook, fasten thine itchy claspe
On some dry Toad-stool that will kindle with thee,
And burn together.

GUARDIANESS
Oh abominable,
Why do you not love me?

CUNNINGAME
No, never did;
I took thee down a little way to
Enforce a Vomit from my offended stomach,
Now thou'rt up agen, I loath thee filthily.

GUARDIANESS
Oh villain.

CUNNINGAME
Why dost thou not see a sight.
Would make a man abjure the sight of Women.

NIECE
Ha, ha, ha, he's vext; ha, ha, ha.

CLOWN
Ha, ha, ha.

NIECE

Why dost thou laugh?

CLOWN
Because thou laugh'st, nothing else i'faith.

CUNNINGAME
She has but mockt my folly, else she finds not
The bosome of my purpose, some other way,
Must make me know; I'll try her, and may chance quit
The fine dexterity of her Lady-wit.

[Exit.

NIECE
Yes introth, I laught to think of thy Master,
Now, what he would think if he knew this?

CLOWN
By my troth I laugh at him too, faith sirrah, he's but a fool to say the truth, though I say't, that should not say't.

NIECE
Yes, thou shouldst say truth, and I believe thee;
Well, for this time we'll part, you perceive something,
Our tongues betray our hearts, there's our weakness,
But pray be silent.

CLOWN
As Mouse in Cheese, or Goose in Hay i'faith.

NIECE
Look, we are cut off, there's my hand where my
Lips would be.

CLOWN
I'll wink, and think 'em thy Lips, farewel.

[Exit.

NIECE
Now Guardianess, I need not ask where you have been.

GUARDIANESS
Oh Lady, never was woman so abus'd.

[Enter **CLOWN**.

CLOWN

Dost thou hear Lady, sweet-heart, I had forgot to tell thee, if you will, I will come back in the evening.

NIECE
By no means, come not till I send for you.

CLOWN
If there be any need, you may think of things when I am gone, I may be convey'd into your chamber, I'll lye under the bed while midnight, or so, or you shall put me up in one of your little boxes, I can creep in at a small hole.

NIECE
These are things I dare not venture, I charge you on my love, never come till I send for you.

CLOWN
Verbum insapienti, 'tis enough to the wise, nor I think it is not fit the Knight should know any thing yet.

NIECE
By no means, pray you go now, we are suspected.

CLOWN
For the things that are past, let us use our secrets.

NIECE
Now I'll make a firm trial of your love,
As you love me, not a word more at this time,
Not a syllable, 'tis the seal of love, take heed.

CLOWN
Hum, hum, hum, hum—.
He humhs loath to depart.

[Exit **CLOWN**.

NIECE
So, this pleasant trouble's gone, now Guardianess,
What? your eyes easing your heart, the cause woman?

GUARDIANESS
The cause is false man, Madam, oh Lady,
I have been gull'd in a shining Carbuncle,
A very Glo-worm, that I thought had fire in't,
And 'tis as cold as Ice.

NIECE
And justly serv'd,
Wouldst thou once think that such an erring spring
Would dote upon thine Autumn?

GUARDIANESS
Oh, had you heard him but protest.

NIECE
I would not have believ'd him,
Thou might'st have perceiv'd how I mock'd thy folly.
In wanton imitation with the Fool,
Go weep the sin of thy credulity,
Not of thy loss, for it was never thine,
And it is gain to miss it; wert thou so dull?
Nay, yet thou'rt stupid and uncapable,
Why, thou wert but the bait to fish with, not
The prey, the stale to catch another Bird with.

GUARDIANESS
Indeed he call'd me Bird.

NIECE
Yet thou perceiv'st not,
It is your Neece he loves, wouldst thou be made
A stalking Jade? 'tis she examine it,
I'll hurry all awry, and tread my path
Over unbeaten grounds, go level to the mark,
Not by circular bouts, rare things are pleasing,
And rare's but seldom in the simple sence,
But has her Emphasis with eminence.

[Exit.

GUARDIANESS
My Neece? she the rival of my abuse?
My flesh and blood wrong me? I'll Aunt her for't;

[Enter **MIRABELL**.

Oh opportunity, thou blessest me
Now Gentlewoman are you parted so soon?
Where's your friend I pray? your Cunningame?

MIRABELL
What say you Aunt?

GUARDIANESS
Come, come, your Cunningame?
I am not blind with age yet, nor deaf.

MIRABELL
Dumb I am sure you are not, what ail you Aunt?

Are you not well?

GUARDIANESS
No, nor sick, nor mad, nor in my wits, nor sleeping, nor waking, nor nothing, nor any thing; I know not what I am, nor what I am not.

MIRABELL
Mercy cover us, what do you mean, Aunt?

GUARDIANESS
I mean to be reveng'd.

MIRABELL
On whom?

GUARDIANESS
On thee Baggage.

MIRABELL
Revenge should follow injury,
Which never reacht so far as thought in me
Towards you Aunt.

GUARDIANESS
Your cunning, minion,
Nor your Cunningame; can either blind me,
The gentle Beggar loves you.

MIRABELL
Beseech you,
Let me stay your error, I begin to hear,
And shake off my amazement; if you think
That ever any passage treating love
Hath been betwixt us yet commenc'd, any
Silent eye-glance that might but sparkle fire,
So much as Brother and Sister might meet with,
The Lip-salute, so much as strangers might
Take a farewel with, the commixed hands,
Nay, but the least thought of the least of these;
In troth you wrong your bosom, by that truth
(Which I think yet you durst be bail for in me,
If it were offer'd ye) I am as free
As all this protestation.

GUARDIANESS
May I believe this?

MIRABELL

If ever you'll believe truth: why, I thought he had spoke love to you, and if his heart prompted his tongue, sure I did hear so much.

GUARDIANESS
Oh falsest man, Ixion's plague fell on me,
Never by woman (such a masculine cloud)
So airy and so subtle was embrac'd.

MIRABELL
By no cause in me, by my life dear Aunt.

GUARDIANESS
I believe you, then help in my revenge,
And you shall do't, or lose my love for ever,
I'll have him quitted at his equal weapon,
Thou art young, follow him, bait his desires
With all the Engines of a womans wit,
Stretch modesty even to the highest pitch;
He cannot freeze at such a flaming beauty;
And when thou hast him by th' amorous gills,
Think on my vengeance, choak up his desires,
Then let his banquetings be Tantalisme,
Let thy disdain spurn the dissembler out;
Oh I should climb my Stars, and sit above,
To see him burn to ashes in his love.

MIRABELL
This will be a strange taste, Aunt, and an
Unwilling labour, yet in your injunction
I am a servant to't.

GUARDIANESS
Thou'lt undertak't?

MIRABELL
Yes, let the success commend it self hereafter.

GUARDIANESS
Effect it Girl, my substance is thy store,
Nothing but want of Will makes woman poor.

[Exeunt.

[Enter **SIR GREGORY** and **CLOWN**.

SIR GREGORY
Why Pompey, thou art not stark mad, art thou?
Wilt thou not tell me how my Lady does?

CLOWN
Your Lady?

SIR GREGORY
Did she receive the thing that I sent her kindly, or no?

CLOWN
The thing that you sent her, Knight, by the thing that you sent, was for the things sake that was sent to carry the thing that you sent, very kindly receiv'd; first, there is your Indenture, now go seek you a servant: secondly, you are a Knight: thirdly and lastly, I am mine own man: and fourthly, fare you well.

SIR GREGORY
Why Pompey? prethee let me speak with thee, I'll lay my life some hare has crost him.

CLOWN
Knight, if you be a Knight, so keep you; as for the Lady, who shall say that she is not a fair Lady, a sweet Lady, an honest and a virtuous Lady, I will say he is a base fellow, a blab of his tongue, and I will make him eat these fingers ends.

SIR GREGORY
Why, here's no body says so Pompey.

CLOWN
Whatsoever things have past between the Lady and the other party, whom I will not name at this time, I say she is virtuous and honest, and I will maintain it, as long as I can maintain my self with bread and water.

SIR GREGORY
Why I know no body thinks otherwise.

CLOWN
Any man that does but think it in my hearing, I will make him think on't while he has a thought in his bosom; shall we say that kindnesses from Ladies are common? or that favours and protestations are things of no moment betwixt parties and parties? I say still, whatsoever has been betwixt the Lady and the party, which I will not name, that she is honest, and shall be honest, whatsoever she does by day or by night, by light or by darkness, with cut and long tail.

SIR GREGORY
Why I say she is honest.

CLOWN
Is she honest? in what sense do you say she is honest, Knight?

SIR GREGORY
If I could not find in my heart to throw my dagger at thy head, hilts and all, I'm an ass, and no Gentleman.

CLOWN

Throw your Dagger at me! do not Knight, I give you fair warning, 'tis but cast away if you do, for you shall have no other words of me, the Lady is an honest Lady, whatsoever reports may go of sports and toys, and thoughts, and words, and deeds, betwixt her and the party which I will not name; this I give you to understand, That another man may have as good an eye, as amorous a nose, as fair a stampt beard, and be as proper a man as a Knight, (I name no parties) a Servingman may be as good as a Sir, a Pompey as a Gregory, a Doodle as a Fop; so Servingman Pompey Doodle, may be respected as well with Ladies (though I name no parties) as Sir Gregory Fop; so farewell:

[Exit.

SIR GREGORY

If the fellow be not out of his wits, then will I never have any more wit while I live; either the sight of the Lady has gaster'd him, or else he's drunk, or else he walks in his sleep, or else he's a fool, or a knave, or both, one of the three, I'm sure 'tis; yet now I think on't, she has not us'd me so kindly as her Uncle promis'd me she should, but that's all one, he says I shall have her, and I dare take his word for the best horse I have, and that's a weightier thing than a Lady, I'm sure on't.

[Exit.

[Enter **LADY RUINOUS**, as a man, **WITTY-PATE**, **SIR RUINOUS**, **PRISCIAN**, and **MASTER CREDULOUS**, binding and robbing her, and in Scarfs. **CREDULOUS** finds the bag.

LADY RUINOUS

Nay, I am your own, 'tis in your pleasure
How you'll deal with me; yet I would intreat,
You will not make that which is bad enough,
Worse than it need be, by a second ill,
When it can render you no second profit;
If it be coin you seek, you have your prey,
All my store I vow, (and it weighs a hundred)
My life, or any hurt you give my body,
Can inrich you no more.

WITTY-PATE

You may pursue.

SIR RUINOUS

As I am a Gentleman; I never will,
Only we'll bind you to quiet behaviour
Till you call out for Bail, and on th' other
Side of the hedge leave you; but keep the peace
Till we be out of hearing, for by that
We shall be out of danger, if we come back,
We come with a mischief.

LADY RUINOUS

You need not fear me.

PRISCIAN
Come, we'll bestow you then.

[Exit **SIR RUINOUS, PRISCIAN** and **LADY RUINOUS.**

WITTY-PATE
Why law you Sir, is not this a swifter Revenue than, Sic probas, ergo's & igitur's can bring in? why is not this one of your Syllogismes in Barbara? Omne utile est honestum.

CREDULOUS
Well Sir, a little more of this acquaintance
Will make me know you fully, I protest.
You have (at first sight) made me conscious
Of such a deed my dreams ne'er prompted, yet
I could almost have wish'd rather ye'ad rob'd me
Of my Cloak, (for my Purse 'tis a Scholars)
Than to have made me a robber.
I had rather have answered three difficult questions,
Than this one, as easie, as yet it seems.

WITTY-PATE
Tush, you shall never come to farther answer for't;
Can you confess your penurious Uncle,
In his full face of love, to be so strict
A Nigard to your Commons, that you are fain
To size your belly out with Shoulder Fees?
With Rumps and Kidneys, and Cues of single Beer,
And yet make Daymy to feed more daintily,
At this easier rate? fie Master Credulous,
I blush for you.

CREDULOUS
This is a truth undeniable.

WITTY-PATE
Why go to then, I hope I know your Uncle,
How does he use his Son, nearer than you?

CREDULOUS
Faith, like his Jade, upon the bare Commons,
Turn'd out to pick his living as he can get it;
He would have been glad to have shar'd in such
A purchase, and thank'd his good fortune too.

[Enter **SIR RUINOUS** and **PRISCIAN.**

But mum no more—is all safe, Bullies?

SIR RUINOUS
Secure, the Gentleman thinks him most happy in his loss,
With his safe life and limbs, and redoubles
His first vow, as he is a Gentleman,
Never to pursue us.

WITTY-PATE
Well away then,
Disperse you with Master Credulous, who still
Shall bear the purchase, Priscian and I,
Will take some other course: You know our meeting
At the Three Cups in St Gile's, with this proviso,
(For 'tis a Law with us) that nothing be open'd
Till all be present, the looser saies a hundred,
And it can weigh no less.

SIR RUINOUS
Come, Sir, we'll be your guide.

CREDULOUS
My honesty, which till now was never forfeited,
All shall be close till our meeting.

[Exit **CREDULOUS** and **SIR RUINOUS**.

WITTY-PATE
Tush, I believ't.
And then all shall out; where's the thief that's robb'd?

[Enter **LADY RUINOUS**.

LADY RUINOUS
Here Master Oldcraft, all follows now.

WITTY-PATE
'Twas neatly done, wench, now to turn that bag
Of counterfeits to current pieces, & actum est.

LADY RUINOUS
You are the Chymist, we'll blow the fire still,
If you can mingle the ingredients.

WITTY-PATE
I will not miss a cause, a quantity, a dram,
You know the place.

PRISCIAN
I have told her that, Sir.

WITTY-PATE
Good, turn Ruinous to be a Constable, I'm sure
We want not beards of all sorts, from the
Worshipful Magistrate to the under Watchman;
Because we must have no danger of life,
But a cleanly cheat, attach Credulous,
The cause is plain, the theft found about him;
Then fall I in his own Cosins shape
By mere accident, where finding him distrest,
I with some difficulty must fetch him off,
With promise that his Uncle shall shut up all
With double restitution: Master Constable, Ruinous
His mouth shall be stopt; you, Mistriss rob-thief,
Shall have your share of what we can gull my Father of;
Is't plain enough?

LADY RUINOUS
As plain a cozenage as can be, faith.

WITTY-PATE
Father, I come again, and again when this is
Past too, Father, one will beget another;
I'd be loath to leave your posterity barren,
You were best to come to composition Father,
Two hundred pieces yearly allow me yet,
It will be cheaper (Father) than my wit,
For I will cheat none but you, dear Father.

[Exeunt.

ACTUS TERTIUS

SCÆNA PRIMA

Enter **SIR PERFIDIOUS**, the Old Knight and **SIR GREGORY**.

SIR PERIFIDIOUS
Why now you take the course Sir Gregory Fop:
I could enforce her, and I list, but love
That's gently won, is a man's own for ever,
Have you prepar'd good Musick?

SIR GREGORY

As fine a noise, Uncle, as heart can wish.

SIR PERFIDIOUS
Why that's done like a Suitor,
They must be woo'd a hundred several ways,
Before you obtain the right way in a woman,
'Tis an odd creature, full of creeks and windings.
The Serpent has not more; for sh'as all his,
And then her own beside came in by her mother.

SIR GREGORY
A fearful portion for a man to venture on.

SIR PERIFIDIOUS
But the way found once by the wits of men,
There is no creature lies so tame agen.

SIR GREGORY
I promise you, not a house-Rabbit, Sir.

SIR PERIFIDIOUS
No sucker on 'em all.

SIR GREGORY
What a thing's that?
They're pretty fools I warrant, when they'r tame
As a man can lay his lips to.

SIR PERIFIDIOUS
How were you bred, Sir?
Did you never make a fool of a Tenants daughter?

SIR GREGORY
Never i'faith, they ha' made some fools for me,
And brought 'em many a time under their aprons.

SIR PERIFIDIOUS
They could not shew you the way plainlier, I think,
To make a fool again.

SIR GREGORY
There's fools enough, Sir,
'Less they were wiser.

SIR PERIFIDIOUS
This is wondrous rare,
Come you to London with a Maiden-head, Knight?
A Gentleman of your rank ride with a Cloak-bag?

Never an Hostess by the way to leave it with?
Nor Tapsters Sister? nor head-Ostlers Wife?
What no body?

SIR GREGORY
Well mock'd old Wit-monger,
I keep it for your Neece.

SIR PERIFIDIOUS
Do not say so for shame, she'll laugh at thee,
A wife ne'er looks for't, 'tis a batchelors penny,
He may giv't to a begger-wench, i'th' progress time,
And ne'er be call'd to account for't.

[Exit.

SIR GREGORY
Would I had known so much,
I could ha' stopt a beggers mouth by th' way.

[Enter **PAGE** and **FIDLERS BOY**.

That rail'd upon me, 'cause I'd give her nothing—
What, are they come?

PAGE
And plac'd directly, Sir,
Under her window.

SIR GREGORY
What may I call you, Gentleman?

BOY
A poor servant to the Viol, I'm the Voice, Sir.

SIR GREGORY
In good time Master Voice?

BOY
Indeed good time does get the mastery.

SIR GREGORY
What Countreyman, Master Voice.

BOY
Sir, born at Ely, we all set up in Ely,
But our house commonly breaks in Rutland-shire.

SIR GREGORY
A shrewd place by my faith, it may well break your voice,
It breaks many a mans back; come, set to your business.

[SONG.

Fain would I wake you, Sweet, but fear
I should invite you to worse chear;
In your dreams you cannot fare
Meaner than Musick; no compare;
None of your slumbers are compil'd
Under the pleasure makes a Child;
Your day-delights, so well compact,
That what you think, turns all to act:
I'd wish my life no better play,
Your dream by night, your thought by day.
Wake gently, wake,
Part softly from your dreams;
The morning flies
To your fair eyes,
To take her special beams.

SIR GREGORY
I hear her up, here Master Voice,
Pay you the Instruments, save what you can,

[Enter **NIECE** above.

To keep you when you're crackt.

[Exit **BOY**.

NIECE
Who should this be?
That I'm so much beholding to, for sweetness?
Pray Heaven it happens right.

SIR GREGORY
Good morrow, Mistriss.

NIECE
An ill day and a thousand come upon thee.

SIR GREGORY
'Light, that's six hundred more than any
Almanack has.

NIECE

Comes it from thee? it is the mangiest Musick
That ever woman heard.

SIR GREGORY
Nay, say not so, Lady,
There's not an itch about 'em.

NIECE
I could curse
My attentive powers, for giving entrance to't;
There is no boldness like the impudence
That's lockt in a fools bloud, how durst you do this?
In conscience I abus'd you as sufficiently
As woman could a man; insatiate Coxcomb,
The mocks and spiteful language I have given thee,
Would o' my life ha' serv'd ten reasonable men,
And rise contented too, and left enough for their friends.
Thou glutton at abuses, never satisfied?
I am perswaded thou devour'st more flouts
Than all thy body's worth, and still a hungred!
A mischief of that maw, prethee seek elsewhere,
Introth I am weary of abusing thee;
Get thee a fresh Mistriss, thou'st make work enough;
I do not think there's scorn enough in Town
To serve thy turn, take the Court-Ladies in,
And all their Women to 'em, that exceed 'em.

SIR GREGORY
Is this in earnest, Lady?

NIECE
Oh unsatiable!
Dost thou count all this but an earnest yet?
I'd thought I'd paid thee all the whole sum, trust me;
Thou'lt begger my derision utterly
If thou stay'st longer, I shall want a laugh:
If I knew where to borrow a contempt
Would hold thee tack, stay and be hang'd, thou shouldst then:
But thou'st no conscience now to extort hate from me,
When one has spent all she can make upon thee;
Must I begin to pay thee hire again?
After I have rid thee twice? faith 'tis unreasonable.

SIR GREGORY
Say you so? I'll know that presently.

[Exit.

NIECE

Now he runs
To fetch my Uncle to this musty bargain,
But I have better ware always at hand.
And lay by this still, when he comes to cheapen.

[Enter **CUNNINGAME**.

CUNNINGAME

I met the Musick now, yet cannot learn
What entertainment he receiv'd from her.

NIECE

There's some body set already, I must to't, I see,
Well, well, Sir Gregory?

CUNNINGAME

Hah, Sir Gregory?

NIECE

Where e'er you come, you may well boast your conquest.

CUNNINGAME

She's lost y'faith, enough, has fortune then
Remembred her great boy? she seldom fails 'em.

NIECE

H' was the unlikeliest man at first, methought,
To have my love, we never met but wrangled.

CUNNINGAME

A pox upon that wrangling, say I still,
I never knew it fail yet, where e'er't came;
It never comes but like a storm of hail,
'Tis sure to bring fine weather at the tail on't,
There's not one match 'mongst twenty made without it,
It fights i' th' tongue, but sure to agree i' th' haunches.

NIECE

That man that should ha' told me when time was.
I should ha' had him, had been laught at piteously,
But see how things will change!

CUNNINGAME

Here's a heart feels it—Oh the deceitful promises of love!
What trust should a man put i' th' lip of woman?
She kist me with that strength, as if sh'ad meant
To ha' set the fair print of her soul upon me.

NIECE
I would ha' sworn 'twould ne'er ha been a match once.

CUNNINGAME
I'll hear no more, I'm mad to hear so much,
Why should I aim my thoughts at better fortunes
Than younger brothers have? that's a Maid with nothing,
Or some old Soap-boilers Widow, without Teeth,
There waits my fortune for me, seek no farther.

[Exit **CUNNINGAME**.

[Enter **SIR PERFIDIOUS**, and **SIR GREGORY**.

SIR PERIFIDIOUS
You tell me things, Sir Gregory, that cannot be.
She will not, nor she dares not.

SIR GREGORY
Would I were whipt then.

NIECE
I'll make as little shew of love, Sir Gregory,
As ever Woman did, you shall not know
You have my heart a good while.

SIR PERIFIDIOUS
Heard you that?

NIECE
Man will insult so soon, 'tis his condition,
'Tis good to keep him off as long as we can,
I've much ado, I swear; and love i' th' end
Will have his course, let Maids do what they can,
They are but frail things till they end in man.

SIR PERIFIDIOUS
What say you to this, Sir?

SIR GREGORY
This is somewhat handsome.

NIECE
And by that little wrangling that I fain'd,
Now I shall try how constant his love is,
Although't went sore against my heart to chide him.

SIR GREGORY
Alas poor Gentlewoman.

SIR PERIFIDIOUS
Now y'are sure of truth,
You hear her own thoughts speak.

SIR GREGORY
They speak indeed.

SIR PERIFIDIOUS
Go, you're a brainless Coax; a Toy, a Fop,
I'll go no farther than your name, Sir Gregory
I'll right my self there; were you from this place,
You should perceive I'm heartily angry with you,
Offer to sow strife 'twixt my Neece and I?
Good morrow Neece, good morrow.

NIECE
Many fair ones to you, Sir.

SIR PERIFIDIOUS
Go, you're a Coxcomb. How dost Neece this morning?
An idle shallow fool: sleep'st thou well, Girl?
Fortune may very well provide thee Lordships,
For honesty has left thee little manners.

SIR GREGORY
How am I bang'd o'both sides!

SIR PERIFIDIOUS
Abuse kindnesse? Will't take the air to day Neece?

NIECE
When you please, Sir,
There stands the Heir behind you I must take,
(Which I'd as lieve take, as take him I swear.)

SIR PERIFIDIOUS
La' you; do you hear't continued to your teeth now?
A pox of all such Gregories; what a hand

[**NIECE** lets fall her Scarfe.

Have I with you!

SIR GREGORY
No more y'feck, I ha' done, Sir:

Lady, your Scarf's fal'n down.

NIECE
'Tis but your luck, Sir,
And does presage the Mistriss must fall shortly,
You may wear it, and you please.

SIR PERIFIDIOUS
There's a trick for you,
You're parlously belov'd, you should complain.

SIR GREGORY
Yes, when I complain, Sir,
Then do your worst, there I'll deceive you, Sir.

SIR PERIFIDIOUS
You are a Dolt, and so I leave you, Sir.

[Exit.

SIR GREGORY
Ah sirrah, Mistriss were you caught, i'faith?
We overheard you all; I must not know
I have your heart, take heed o' that, I pray,
I knew some Scarf would come.

NIECE
He's quite gone, sure:
Ah you base Coxcomb, couldst thou come again?
And so abus'd as thou wast?

SIR GREGORY
How?

NIECE
'Twould ha' kill'd
A sensible man, he would ha' gone to his chamber,
And broke his heart by this time.

SIR GREGORY
Thank you heartily.

NIECE
Or fixt a naked Rapier in a Wall,
Like him that earn'd his Knighthood, e'r he had it,
And then refus'd upon't, ran up to th' hilts.

SIR GREGORY

Yes, let him run for me, I was never brought up to't,
I never profest running i' my life.

NIECE
What art thou made on? thou tough villanous vermin.
Will nothing destroy thee?

SIR GREGORY
Yes, yes, assure your self
Unkind words may do much.

NIECE
Why, dost thou want 'em?
I've e'en consum'd my spleen to help thee to 'em:
Tell me what sort of words they be would speed thee?
I'll see what I can do yet.

SIR GREGORY
I'm much beholding to you,
You're willing to bestow huge pains upon me.

NIECE
I should account nothing too much to rid thee.

SIR GREGORY
I wonder you'd not offer to destroy me,
All the while your Uncle was here.

NIECE
Why there thou betray'st thy house; we of the Old-Crafts
Were born to more wit than so.

SIR GREGORY
I wear your favor here.

NIECE
Would it might rot thy arme off: if thou knewst
With what contempt thou hast it, what hearts bitterness,
How many cunning curses came along with it,
Thoud'st quake to handle it.

SIR GREGORY
A pox, tak't again then;
Who'd be thus plagu'd of all hands?

NIECE
No, wear't still,
But long I hope thou shalt not, 'tis but cast

Upon thee, purposely to serve another
That has more right to't, as in some Countries they convey
Their treasure upon Asses to their friends;
If mine be but so wise, and apprehensive,
As my opinion gives him to my heart,
It stayes not long on thy desertless arme;
I'll make thee e'er I ha' done, not dare to wear
Any thing of mine, although I give't thee freely;
Kiss it you may, and make what shew you can,
But sure you carry't to a worthier Man,
And so good morrow to you.

[Exit.

SIR GREGORY
Hu hum, ha hum;
I han't the spirit now to dash my brains out,
Nor the audacity to kill my self,
But I could cry my heart out, that's as good,
For so't be out, no matter which way it comes,
If I can dye with a fillip, or depart
At hot-cockles, What's that to any man?
If there be so much death that serves my turn there.
Every one knows the state of his own body,
No Carrion kills a Kite, but then agen
There's Cheese will choak a Daw; time I were dead I'faith,
If I knew which way without hurt or danger.
I am a Maiden-Knight, and cannot look
Upon a naked weapon with any modesty,
Else 'twould go hard with me, and to complain
To Sir Perfidious the old Knight agen,
Were to be more abus'd; perhaps he would beat me well,
But ne'er believe me.

[Enter **CUNNINGAME**.

And few Men dye o' beating, that were lost too:
Oh, here's my friend, I'll make my moan to him.

CUNNINGAME
I cannot tear her memory from my heart,
That treads mine down, was ever man so fool'd
That profest wit?

SIR GREGORY
O Cunningame?

CUNNINGAME

Sir Gregory?
The choice, the Victor, the Towns happy Man?

SIR GREGORY
'Snigs, What do'st mean? come I to thee for comfort, and do'st abuse me too?

CUNNINGAME
Abuse you? How Sir?
With justifying your fortune, and your joyes?

SIR GREGORY
Pray hold your hand, Sir, I've been bob'd enough,
You come with a new way now; strike me merrily,
But when a man's sore beaten o' both sides already,
Then the least tap in jest goes to the guts on him;
Wilt ha the truth? I'm made the rankest ass
That e'er was born to Lordships.

CUNNINGAME
What? No Sir?

SIR GREGORY
I had not thought my body could a yielded
All those foul scurvie names that she has call'd me,
I wonder whence she fetcht 'em?

CUNNINGAME
Is this credible?

SIR GREGORY
She pin'd this Scarf upon me afore her Unckle,
But his back turn'd, she curst me so for wearing on't,
The very brawn of mine arme has ak'd ever since,
Yet in a manner forc't me to wear't still,
But hop't I should not long; if good luck serve
I should meet one that has more wit and worth
Should take it from me, 'twas but lent to me,
And sent to him for a token.

CUNNINGAME
I conceit it, I know the Man
That lies in wait for't, part with't by all means,
In any case, you are way-laid about it.

SIR GREGORY
How Sir? way-laid?

CUNNINGAME

Pox of a Scarf, say I,
I prize my friends life 'bove a million on 'em,
You shall be rul'd, Sir, I know more than you.

SIR GREGORY
If you know more than I, let me be rid on't,
'Lass, 'tis not for my wearing, so she told me.

CUNNINGAME
No, no, give me't, the knave shall miss his purpose,
And you shall live.

SIR GREGORY
I would, as long as I could, Sir.

CUNNINGAME
No more replyes, you shall, I'll prevent this,
Pompey shall march without it.

SIR GREGORY
What, is't he?
My Man that was?

CUNNINGAME
Call him your deadly Enemy;
You give him too fair a name, you deal too nobly,
He bears a bloody mind, a cruel foe, Sir,
I care not if he heard me.

SIR GREGORY
But, Do you hear, Sir?
Can't sound with reason she should affect him?

CUNNINGAME
Do you talk of reason? I never thought to have heard
Such a word come from you; reason in love?
Would you give that, no Doctor could e'er give?
Has not a Deputy married his Cook-maid?
An Aldermans Widow, one that was her turn-broach?
Nay, Has not a great Lady brought her Stable
Into her Chamber: lay with her Horse-keeper?

SIR GREGORY
Did ever love play such Jades tricks, Sir?

CUNNINGAME
Oh thousands, thousands: Beware a sturdy Clown e're
while you live, Sir;

'Tis like a huswifery in most Shires about us;
You shall ha' Farmers Widows wed thin Gentlemen,
Much like your self, but put'em to no stress;
What work can they do, with small trap-stick legs?
They keep Clowns to stop gaps, and drive in pegs,
A drudgery fit for Hindes, e'en back agen, Sir,
Your're safest at returning.

SIR GREGORY
Think you so, Sir?

CUNNINGAME
But, How came this Clown to be call'd Pompey first?

SIR GREGORY
Push, one good-man Cæsar, a Pump-maker kersen'd him;
Pompey he writes himself, but his right name's Pumpey,
And stunk too when I had him, now he's crank.

CUNNINGAME
I'm glad I know so much to quell his pride, Sir,
Walk you still that way, I'll make use of this,
To resolve all my doubts, and place this favor
On some new Mistriss, only for a try,
And if it meet my thoughts, I'll swear 'tis I.

[Exit.

SIR GREGORY
Is Pompey grown so malepert? so frampel?
The onely cutter about Ladies honors?

[Enter **SIR PERFIDIOUS**, the Old Knight.

And his blade soonest out?

SIR PERFIDIOUS
Now, What's the news, Sir?

SIR GREGORY
I dare not say but good; oh excellent good, Sir.

SIR PERFIDIOUS
I hope now you're resolv'd she loves you, Knight?

SIR GREGORY
Cuds me, What else Sir? that's not to do now.

SIR PERFIDIOUS
You would not think how desperately you anger'd me,
When you bely'd her goodness; oh you vext me,
Even to a Palsey.

SIR GREGORY
What a thing was that Sir?

[Enter **NIECE**.

NIECE
'Tis, that 'tis; as I have hope of sweetness, the
Scarfe's gone;
Worthy wise friend, I doat upon thy cunning,
We two shall be well matcht, our Issue-male, sure
Will be born Counsellors; is't possible?
Thou shalt have another token out of hand for't;
Nay, since the way's found, pitty thou shouldst want, y'faith,
O my best joy, and dearest.

SIR PERFIDIOUS
Well said, Neece,
So violent 'fore your Uncle? What will you do
In secret then?

SIR GREGORY
Marry call me slave, and rascal.

NIECE
Your Scarfe—the Scarfe I gave you—

SIR PERFIDIOUS
Mass that's true Neece,
I ne'er thought upon that; the Scarfe she gave you—Sir?
What dumb? No answer from you? the Scarfe?

SIR GREGORY
I was way-laid about it, my life threatned;
Life's life, Scarfe's but a Scarfe, and so I parted from't.

NIECE
Unfortunate woman! my first favor too?

SIR PERFIDIOUS
Will you be still an ass? no reconcilement
'Twixt you and wit? Are you so far fallen out,
You'l never come together? I tell you true,
I'm very lowsily asham'd on you,

That's the worst shame that can be;
Thus bayting on him: now his heart's hook't in,
I'll make him, e'er I ha' done, take her with nothing,
I love a man that lives by his wits alife;
Nay leave, sweet Neece, 'tis but a Scarfe, let it go.

NIECE
The going of it never grieves me, Sir.
It is the manner, the manner—

SIR GREGORY
O dissembling Marmaset! If I durst speak,
Or could be believ'd when I speak,
What a tale could I tell, to make hair stand upright now!

NIECE
Nay, Sir, at your request you shall perceive, Uncle,
With what renewing love I forgive this:
Here's a fair Diamond, Sir, I'll try how long
You can keep that.

SIR GREGORY
Not very long, you know't too,
Like a cunning witch as you are.

NIECE
Y'are best let him ha' that too.

SIR GREGORY
So I were, I think, there were no living else,
I thank you, as you have handled the matter.

SIR PERFIDIOUS
Why this is musical now, and Tuesday next
Shall tune your Instruments, that's the day set.

NIECE
A match, good Uncle.

SIR PERFIDIOUS
Sir, you hear me too?

SIR GREGORY
Oh very well, I'm for you.

NIECE
What e'er you hear, you know my mind.

[Exeunt **SIR PERFIDIOUS** and **NIECE**.

SIR GREGORY

I, a pox on't, too well, if I do not wonder how we two shall come together, I'm a Bear whelp? he talks of Tuesday next, as familiarly, as if we lov'd one another, but 'tis as unlikely to me, as 'twas seven year before I saw her; I shall try his cunning, it may be he has a way was never yet thought on, and it had need to be such a one, for all that I can think on will never do't; I look to have this Diamond taken from me very speedily, therefore I'll take it off o' my finger, for if it be seen, I shall be way-laid for that too.

[Exit.

ACTUS QUARTUS

SCÆNA PRIMA

Enter **SIR PERFIDIOUS**, and **WITTY-PATE**.

SIR PERFIDIOUS

Oh torture! torture! thou carriest a sting i'thy tail,
Thou never brought'st good news i'thy life yet,
And that's an ill quality, leave it when thou wilt.

WITTY-PATE

Why you receive a blessing the wrong way, Sir,
Call you not this good newes? to save at once Sir
Your credit and your kinsmans life together;
Would it not vex your peace, and gaule your worth?
T'have one of your name hang'd?

SIR PERFIDIOUS

Peace, no such words, boy.

WITTY-PATE

Be thankful for the blessing of prevention then.

SIR PERFIDIOUS

Le' me see, there was none hang'd out of our house since Brute,
I ha' search't both Stow, and Hollinshead.

WITTY-PATE

O Sir.

SIR PERFIDIOUS

I'll see what Polychronicon sayes anon too.

WITTY-PATE

'Twas a miraculous fortune that I heard on't.

SIR PERFIDIOUS
I would thou'dst never heard on't.

WITTY-PATE
That's true too,
So it had ne'er been done; to see the luck on't,
He was ev'n brought to Justice Aurums threshold,
There had flew'n forth a Mittimus straight for Newgate;
And note the fortune too, Sessions a Thursday,
Jury cull'd out a Friday, Judgment a Saturday,
Dungeon a Sunday, Tyburne a Munday,
Miseries quotidian ague, when't begins once,
Every day pulls him, till he pull his last.

SIR PERFIDIOUS
No more, I say, 'tis an ill theam: where left you him?

WITTY-PATE
He's i'th' Constables hands below i'th' Hall, Sir,
Poor Gentleman, and his accuser with him.

SIR PERFIDIOUS
What's he?

WITTY-PATE
A Judges Son 'tis thought, so much the worse too,
He'l hang his enemy, an't shall cost him nothing,
That's a great priviledge.

SIR PERFIDIOUS
Within there?

[Enter **SERVANT**.

SERVANT
Sir?

SIR PERFIDIOUS
Call up the folks i'th' Hall. I had such hope on him,
For a Scholar too, a thing thou ne'er wast fit for
Therefore erected all my joyes in him;
Got a Welch Benefice in reversion for him,
Dean of Cardigan, has his grace already,
He can marry and bury, yet ne'er a hair on's face;

[Enter **CREDULOUS**, **SIR RUINOUS**, as a Constable, and **LADY GENTRY**, as a Man.

Like a French Vicar, and,
Does he bring such fruits to Town with him?
A Thief at his first lighting?
Oh good den to you.

WITTY-PATE
Nay, sweet Sir, you'r so vext now, you'l grieve him,
And hurt your self.

SIR PERFIDIOUS
Away, I'll hear no counsel;
Come you but once in seven year to your Uncle,
And at that time must you be brought home too?
And by a Constable?

WITTY-PATE
Oh speak low, Sir,
Remember your own credit, you profess
You love a Man o'wit, begin at home, Sir,
Express it i'your self.

LADY
Nay, Master Constable,
Shew your self a wise man, 'gainst your nature too.

SIR RUINOUS
Sir, no Dish-porridgment, we have brought home
As good men as ye.

SIR PERFIDIOUS
Out, a North-Brittain Constable, that tongue
Will publish all, it speaks so broad already;
Are you the Gentleman.

LADY
The unfortunate one, Sir,
That fell into the power of merciless Thieves,
Whereof this fellow, whom I'd call your kinsman,
As little as I could (for the fair reverence
I owe to fame and years) was the prime villain.

SIR PERFIDIOUS
A wicked prime.

WITTY-PATE
Nay, not so loud, sweet father.

LADY
The rest are fled, but I shall meet with 'em,
Hang one of 'em I will certain, I ha' swore it,
And 'twas my luck to light upon this first.

SIR PERFIDIOUS
A Cambridge man for this? these your degrees, Sir?
Nine years at University for this fellowship?

WITTY-PATE
Take your voice lower, dear Sir.

SIR PERFIDIOUS
What's your loss, Sir?

LADY
That which offends me to repeat, the Money's whole, Sir,
'Tis i'th' Constables hands there, a seal'd hundred,
But I will not receive it.

SIR PERFIDIOUS
No? Not the Money, Sir,
Having confest 'tis all?

LADY
'Tis all the Money, Sir,
But 'tis not all I lost, for when they bound me,
They took a Diamond hung at my shirt string,
Which fear of life made me forget to hide;
It being the sparkling witness of a Contract,
'Twixt a great Lawyers daughter and my self.

WITTY-PATE
I told you what he was; What does the Diamond
Concern my Cozen, Sir?

LADY
No more did the Money,
But he shall answer all now.

WITTY-PATE
There's your conscience,
It shewes from whence you sprung.

LADY
Sprung? I had leapt a Thief,
Had I leapt some of your alliance.

WITTY-PATE
Slave!

LADY
You prevent me still.

SIR PERFIDIOUS
'Slid, Son, Are you mad?

LADY
Come, come, I'll take a legal course.

SIR PERFIDIOUS
Will you undo us all? What's your demand, Sir?
Now we're in's danger too.

LADY
A hundred Mark, Sir,
I will not bait a doit.

WITTY-PATE
A hundred Rascals.

LADY
Sir, find 'em out in your own blood, and take 'em.

WITTY-PATE
Go take your course, follow the Law, and spare not.

SIR PERFIDIOUS
Does fury make you drunk? know you what you say?

WITTY-PATE
A hundred dogs dungs, do your worst.

SIR PERFIDIOUS
You do I'm sure; Whose loud now?

WITTY-PATE
What his own asking?

SIR PERFIDIOUS
Not in such a case?

WITTY-PATE
You shall have but threescore pound; spite a your teeth,
I'll see you hang'd first.

SIR PERFIDIOUS
And what's seven pound more man?
That all this coyle's about? stay, I say, he shall ha't.

WITTY-PATE
It is your own, you may do what you please with it;
Pardon my zeal, I would ha' sav'd you money;
Give him all his own asking?

SIR PERFIDIOUS
What's that to you, Sir?
Be sparing of your own, teach me to pinch
In such a case as this? go, go, live by your wits, go.

WITTY-PATE
I practise all I can.

SIR PERFIDIOUS
Follow you me, Sir,
And, Master Constable, come from the knave,
And be a witness of a full recompence.

WITTY-PATE
Pray stop the Constables mouth, what ere you do Sir.

SIR PERFIDIOUS
Yet agen? as if I meant not to do that my self,
Without your counsel? As for you, precious kinsman,
Your first years fruits in Wales shall go to rack for this,
You lie not in my house, I'll pack you out,
And pay for your lodging rather.

[Exeunt **SIR PERFIDIOUS, SIR RUINOUS** and **LADY.**

WITTY-PATE
Oh fie Cozen,
These are ill courses, you a Scholar too?

CREDULOUS
I was drawn into't most unfortunately,
By filthy deboist company.

WITTY-PATE
I, I, I.
'Tis even the spoil of all our youth in England.
What were they Gentlemen?

CREDULOUS

Faith so like some on 'em,
They were ev'n the worse agen.

WITTY-PATE
Hum.

CREDULOUS
Great Tobacco swivers,
They would go near to rob with a pipe in their mouths.

WITTY-PATE
What, no?

CREDULOUS
Faith leave it Cozen, because my Rascals use it.

WITTY-PATE
So they do meat and drink, must worthy Gentlemen
Refrain their food for that? an honest man
May eat of the same Pig some Parson dines with,
A Lawyer and a fool feed of one Woodcock,
Yet one ne'er the simpler, t'other ne'er the wiser;
'Tis not meat, drink, or smoak, dish, cup, or pipe,
Co-operates to the making of a Knave,
'Tis the condition makes a slave, a slave,
There's London Philosophy for you; I tell you Cozen,
You cannot be too cautelous, nice, or dainty,
In your society here, especially
When you come raw from the University,
Before the World has hard'ned you a little,
For as a butter'd loaf is a Scholars breakfast there,
So a poach't Scholar is a cheaters dinner here,
I ha' known seven of 'em supt up at a Meale.

CREDULOUS
Why a poacht Scholar?

WITTY-PATE
'Cause he powres himself forth,
And all his secrets, at the first acquaintance,
Never so crafty to be eaten i'th' shell,
But is outstript of all he has at first,
And goes down glib, he's swallowed with sharp wit,
Stead of Wine Vinegar.

CREDULOUS
I shall think, Cozen,
O' your poach't Scholar, while I live.

[Enter **SERVANT**.

SERVANT
Master Credulous,
Your Uncle wills you to forbear the House,
You must with me, I'm charg'd to see you plac'd
In some new lodging about Theeving Lane,
What the conceit's, I know not, but commands you
To be seen here no more, till you hear further.

CREDULOUS
Here's a strange welcome, Sir.

WITTY-PATE
This is the World, Cozen;
When a Man's fame's once poyson'd, fare thee well Lad.

[Exit **CREDULOUS** and **SERVANT**.

This is the happiest cheat I e'er claim'd share in,
It has a two-fold fortune, gets me coyne,
And puts him out of grace, that stood between me,
My fathers Cambridge Jewel, much suspected
To be his Heir, now there's a bar in's hopes.

[Enter **SIR RUINOUS** and **LADY GENTRY**.

SIR RUINOUS
It chinks, make haste.

LADY
The Goat at Smithfield Pens.

[Enter **CUNNINGAME**.

WITTY-PATE
Zo, zo, zufficient. Master Cunningame?
I never have ill luck when I meet a wit.

CUNNINGAME
A Wit's better to meet, than to follow then,
For I ha' none so good I can commend yet,
But commonly men unfortunate to themselves,
Are luckiest to their friends, and so may I be.

WITTY-PATE
I run o'er so much worth, going but in haste from you,

All my deliberate friendship cannot equal.

CUNNINGAME
'Tis but to shew, that you can place sometimes,

[Enter **MIRABELL**.

Your modesty a top of all your virtues.

[Exit **WITTY-PATE**.

This Gentleman may pleasure me yet agen;
I am so haunted with this broad-brim'd hat,
Of the last progress block, with the young hat-band,
Made for a sucking Devil of two years old,
I know not where to turn my self.

MIRABELL
Sir?

CUNNINGAME
More torture?

MIRABELL
'Tis rumor'd that you love me.

CUNNINGAME
A my troth Gentlewoman,
Rumor's as false a knave as ever pist then,
Pray tell him so from me; I cannot fain
With a sweet Gentlewoman, I must deal down right.

MIRABELL
I heard, though you dissembled with my Aunt, Sir,
And that makes me more confident.

CUNNINGAME
There's no falshood,
But payes us our own some way, I confess
I Fain'd with her, 'twas for a weightier purpose,
But not with thee, I swear.

MIRABELL
Nor I with you then,
Although my Aunt enjoyn'd me to dissemble,
To right her splene, I love you faithfully.

CUNNINGAME

Light, this is worse than 'twas.

MIRABELL
I find such worth in you,
I cannot, nay I dare not dally with you,
For fear the flame consume me.

CUNNINGAME
Here's fresh trouble,
This drives me to my conscience, for 'tis foul
To injure one that deals directly with me.

MIRABELL
I crave but such a truth from your love, Sir,
As mine brings you, and that's proportionable.

CUNNINGAME
A good Geometrician, 'shrew my heart;
Why are you out o'your wits, pretty plump Gentlewoman,
You talk so desperately? 'tis a great happiness,
Love has made one on's wiser than another,
We should be both cast away else;
Yet I love gratitude, I must requite you,
I shall be sick else, but to give you me,
A thing you must not take, if you mean to live,
For a' my troth I hardly can my self;
No wise Physitian will prescribe me for you.
Alass, your state is weak, you had need of Cordials,
Some rich Electuary, made of a Son an Heir,
An elder brother, in a Cullisse, whole,
'Tmust be some wealthy Gregory, boyl'd to a Jelly,
That must restore you to the state of new Gowns,
French Ruffs, and mutable head-tires.

MIRABELL
But, Where is he, Sir?
One that's so rich will ne'er wed me with nothing.

CUNNINGAME
Then see thy Conscience, and thy wit together,
Would'st thou have me then, that has nothing neither?
What say you to Fop Gregory the first, yonder?
Will you acknowledge your time amply recompenc'd?
Full satisfaction upon loves record?
Without any more suit, if I combine you?

MIRABELL
Yes, by this honest kiss.

CUNNINGAME

You're a wise Clyent,
To pay your fee before-hand, but all do so,
You know the worst already, that's the best too.

MIRABELL

I know he's a fool.

CUNNINGAME

You'r shrewdly hurt then;
This is your comfort, your great wisest Women
Pick their first Husband still out of that house,
And some will have 'em to chuse, if they bury twenty.

MIRABELL

I'm of their minds, that like him for a first Husband,
To run youths race with him, 'tis very pleasant,
But when I'm old, I'd alwayes wish for a wiser.

CUNNINGAME

You may have me by that time:
For this first business,
Rest upon my performance.

MIRABELL

With all thankfulness.

CUNNINGAME

I have a project you must aid me in too.

MIRABELL

You bind me to all lawful action, Sir.

CUNNINGAME

Pray wear this Scarf about you.

MIRABELL

I conjecture now—

CUNNINGAME

There's a Court Principle for't, one office must help another;
As for example, for your cast o' Manchits out o'th' Pantry,
I'll allow you a Goose out o'th' Kitchin.

MIRABELL

'Tis very sociably done, Sir, farewel performance,
I shall be bold to call you so.

CUNNINGAME
Do, sweet confidence,

[Enter **SIR GREGORY**.

If I can match my two broad brim'd hats;
'Tis he, I know the Maggot by his head;
Now shall I learn newes of him, my precious chief.

SIR GREGORY
I have been seeking for you i'th' bowling-Green,
Enquir'd at Nettletons, and Anthonies Ordinary,
T'ha's vext me to the heart, look, I've a Diamond here,
And it cannot find a Master.

CUNNINGAME
No? That's hard y'faith.

SIR GREGORY
It does belong to some body, a pox on him,
I would he had it, do's but trouble me,
And she that sent it, is so waspish too,
There's no returning to her till't be gone.

CUNNINGAME
Oh, ho, ah sirrah, are you come?

SIR GREGORY
What's that friend?

CUNNINGAME
Do you note that corner sparkle?

SIR GREGORY
Which? which? which Sir?

CUNNINGAME
At the West end o'th' Coller.

SIR GREGORY
Oh I see't now.

CUNNINGAME
'Tis an apparent mark; this is the stone, Sir,
That so much blood is threatned to be shed for.

SIR GREGORY

I pray.

CUNNINGAME
A tun at least.

SIR GREGORY
They must not find't i'me then, they must
Goe where 'tis to be had.

CUNNINGAME
'Tis well it came to my hands first, Sir Gregory,
I know where this must go.

SIR GREGORY
Am I discharg'd on't?

CUNNINGAME
My life for yours now.

[Draws.

SIR GREGORY
What now?

CUNNINGAME
'Tis discretion, Sir,
I'll stand upon my Guard all the while I ha't.

SIR GREGORY
'Troth thou tak'st too much danger on thee still,
To preserve me alive.

CUNNINGAME
'Tis a friends duty, Sir,
Nay, by a toy that I have late thought upon,
I'll undertake to get your Mistriss for you.

SIR GREGORY
Thou wilt not? Wilt?

CUNNINGAME
Contract her by a trick, Sir,
When she least thinks on't.

SIR GREGORY
There's the right way to't,
For if she think on't once, shee'l never do't.

CUNNINGAME
She does abuse you still then?

SIR GREGORY
A pox! damnably,
Every time worse than other; yet her Uncle
Thinks the day holds a Tuesday; say it did, Sir,
She's so familiarly us'd to call me Rascal,
She'll quite forget to wed me by my own name,
And then that Marriage cannot hold in Law, you know.

CUNNINGAME
Will you leave all to me?

SIR GREGORY
Who should I leave it to?

CUNNINGAME
'Tis our luck to love Neeces; I love a Neece too.

SIR GREGORY
I would you did y'faith.

CUNNINGAME
But mine's a kind wretch.

SIR GREGORY
I marry Sir, I would mine were so too.

CUNNINGAME
No rascal comes in her mouth.

SIR GREGORY
Troth, and mine has little else in hers.

CUNNINGAME
Mine sends me tokens,
All the World knows not on.

SIR GREGORY
Mine gives me tokens too, very fine tokens,
But I dare not wear 'em.

CUNNINGAME
Mine's kind in secret.

SIR GREGORY
And there mine's a hell-cat.

CUNNINGAME
We have a day set too.

SIR GREGORY
'Slid, so have we man,
But there's no sign of ever coming together.

CUNNINGAME
I'll tell thee who 'tis, the old womans Neece.

SIR GREGORY
Is't she?

CUNNINGAME
I would your luck had been no worse for mildness;
But mum, no more words on't to your Lady.

SIR GREGORY
Foh!

CUNNINGAME
No blabbing, as you love me.

SIR GREGORY
None of our blood
Were ever bablers.

CUNNINGAME
Prethee convey this Letter to her,
But at any hand let not your Mistriss see't.

SIR GREGORY
Yet agen Sir?

CUNNINGAME
There's a Jewel in't,
The very art would make her doat upon't.

SIR GREGORY
Say you so?
And she shall see't for that trick only.

CUNNINGAME
Remember but your Mistriss, and all's well.

SIR GREGORY
Nay, if I do not, hang me.

[Exit.

CUNNINGAME
I believe you;
This is the onely way to return a token,
I know he will do't now, 'cause he's charg'd to'th' contrary.
He's the nearest kin to a Woman, of a thing
Made without substance, that a man can find agen,
Some Petticoat begot him, I'll be whipt else,
Engendring with an old pair of paund hose,
Lying in some hot chamber o'er the Kitchin:
Very steame bred him,
He never came where Rem in Re e'er grew;
The generation of a hundred such
Cannot make a man stand in a white sheet,
For 'tis no act in Law, nor can a Constable
Pick out a bawdy business for Bridewell in't;

[Enter **CLOWN**, as a Gallant.

A lamentable case, he's got with a Mans Urine, like a Mandrake.
How now? hah? What prodigious bravery's this?
A most preposterous Gallant, the Doublet sits
As if it mock't the breeches.

CLOWN
Save you, Sir.

CUNNINGAME
H'as put his tongue in the fine suit of words too.

CLOWN
How does the party?

CUNNINGAME
Takes me for a Scrivener. Which of the parties?

CLOWN
Hum, simplicity betide thee—
I would fain hear of the party; I would be loath to go
Farther with her; honor is not a thing to be dallied withall,
No more is reputation, no nor fame, I take it, I must not
Have her wrong'd when I'm abroad; my party is not
To be compell'd with any party in an oblique way;
'Tis very dangerous to deal with Women;
May prove a Lady too, but shall be nameless,
I'll bite my tongue out, e'er it prove a Traitor.

CUNNINGAME
Upon my life I know her.

CLOWN
Not by me,
Know what you can, talk a whole day with me,
Y'are ne'er the wiser, she comes not from these lips.

CUNNINGAME
The old Knights Neece.

CLOWN
'Slid he has got her, pox of his heart that told him,
Can nothing be kept secret? let me entreat you
To use her name as little as you can, though.

CUNNINGAME
'Twill be small pleasure, Sir, to use her name.

CLOWN
I had intelligence in my solemn walks,
'Twixt Paddington and Pancridge, of a Scarfe,
Sent for a token, and a Jewel follow'd,
But I acknowledge not the receipt of any,
How e'er 'tis carried, believe me, Sir,
Upon my reputation I receiv'd none.

CUNNINGAME
What, neither Scarfe nor Jewel?

CLOWN
'Twould be seen
Some where about me, you may well think that,
I have an arme for a Scarfe, as others have,
An Ear, to hang a Jewel too, and that's more
Then some men have, my betters a great deal,
I must have restitution, where e'er it lights.

CUNNINGAME
And reason good.

CLOWN
For all these tokens, Sir,
Pass i' my name.

CUNNINGAME
It cannot otherwise be.

CLOWN
Sent to a worthy friend.

CUNNINGAME
I, that's to thee.

CLOWN
I'm wrong'd under that title.

CUNNINGAME
I dare sware thou art,
'Tis nothing but Sir Gregories circumvention,
His envious spite, when thou'rt at Paddington,
He meets the gifts at Pancridge.

CLOWN
Ah false Knight?
False both to honor, and the Law of Arms?

CUNNINGAME
What wilt thou say if I be reveng'd for thee?
Thou sit as Witness?

CLOWN
I should laugh in state then.

CUNNINGAME
I'll fob him, here's my hand.

CLOWN
I shall be as glad as any Man alive, to see him well fob'd, Sir; but now you talk of fobbing, I wonder the Lady sends not for me according to promise? I ha' kept out o' Town these two dayes, a purpose to be sent for; I am almost starv'd with walking.

CUNNINGAME
Walking gets men a stomach.

CLOWN
'Tis most true, Sir, I may speak it by experience, for I ha' got a stomach six times, and lost it agen, as often as a traveller from Chelsy shall lose the sight of Pauls, and get it agen.

CUNNINGAME
Go to her, Man.

CLOWN
Not for a Million, enfringe my oath? there's a toy call'd a Vow, has past between us, a poor trifle, Sir; Pray do me the part and office of a Gentleman, if you chance to meet a Footman by the way, in Orange

tawny ribbands, running before an empty Coach, with a Buzard i'th' Poop on't, direct him and his horses toward the new River by Islington, there they shall have me looking upon the Pipes, and whistling.

[Exit **CLOWN**.

CUNNINGAME
A very good note; this love makes us all Monkeyes,
But to my work: 'Scarfe first? and now a Diamond?
These should be sure signs of her affections truth;
Yet I'll go forward with my surer proof:

[Exit.

[Enter **NIECE**, and **SIR GREGORY**.

NIECE
Is't possible?

SIR GREGORY
Nay, here's his Letter too, there's a fine Jewel in't,
Therefore I brought it to you.

NIECE
You tedious Mongril! Is't not enough
To grace thee, to receive this from thy hand,
A thing which makes me almost sick to do,
But you must talk too?

SIR GREGORY
I ha' done.

NIECE
Fall back,
Yet backer, backer yet, you unmannerly puppy,
Do you not see I'm going about to read it?

SIR GREGORY
Nay, these are golden dayes, now I stay by't,
She was wont not to endure me in her sight at all,
The World mends, I see that.

NIECE
What an ambiguous Superscription's here!
To the best of Neeces. Why that title may be mine,
And more than her's:
Sure I much wrong the neatness of his art;
'Tis certain sent to me, and to requite
My cunning in the carriage of my Tokens,

Us'd the same Fop for his.

SIR GREGORY
She nodded now to me, 'twill come in time.

NIECE
What's here? an entire Rubye, cut into a heart,
And this the word, Istud Amoris opus?

SIR GREGORY
Yes, yes, I have heard him say, that love is
the best stone-cutter.

NIECE
Why thou sawcy issue of some travelling Sow-gelder,
What makes love in thy mouth? Is it a thing
That ever will concern thee? I do wonder
How thou dar'st think on't! hast thou ever hope
To come i' the same roome where lovers are;
And scape unbrain'd with one of their velvet slippers?

SIR GREGORY
Love tricks break out I see, and you talk of slippers once,
'Tis not far off to bed time.

NIECE
Is it possible thou canst laugh yet?
I would ha' undertook to ha' kill'd a spider
With less venome far, than I have spit at thee.

SIR GREGORY
You must conceive,
A Knight's another manner a piece of flesh.

NIECE
Back, Owles-face.

SIR PERFIDIOUS [Within]
Do, do.

NIECE
'Tis my Unckles voice, that.
Why keep you so far off, Sir Gregory?
Are you afraid, Sir, to come near your Mistriss?

SIR GREGORY
Is the proud heart come down? I lookt for this still.

NIECE

He comes not this way yet: Away, you dog-whelp,
Would you offer to come near me, though I said so?
I'll make you understand my mind in time;
Your running greedily, like a hound to his breakfast,
That chops in head and all to beguile his fellows;
I'm to be eaten, Sir, with Grace and leisure,
Behaviour and discourse, things that ne'er trouble you;
After I have pelted you sufficiently,
I tro you will learn more manners.

SIR GREGORY

I'm wondring still when we two shall come together?
Tuesday's at hand, but I'm as far off, as I was at first, I swear.

[Enter **GUARDIANESS**.

GUARDIANESS

Now Cunningame, I'll be reveng'd at large:
Lady, what was but all this while suspition,
Is truth, full blown now, my Neece wears your Scarfe.

NIECE

Hah?

GUARDIANESS

Do but follow me, I'll place you instantly
Where you shall see her courted by Cunningame.

NIECE

I go with greediness; we long for things
That break our hearts sometimes, there's pleasures misery,

[Exeunt **NIECE** and **GUARDIANESS**.

SIR GREGORY

Where are those gad-flies going? to some Junket now;
That some old bumble-bee toles the young one forth
To sweet meats after kind, let 'em look to't,
The thing you wot on be not mist or gone,
I bring a Maiden-head, and I look for one.
Which is only a Puppet so drest.

[Exit.

[Enter **CUNNINGAME**, in discourse with a Mask't **GENTLEWOMAN** in a broad hat, and scarf'd, **NIECE** at another door.

CUNNINGAME
Yes, yes.

NIECE
Too manifest now, the Scarfe and all.

CUNNINGAME
It cannot be, you're such a fearful soul.

NIECE
I'll give her cause of fear e'er I part from her.

CUNNINGAME
Will you say so? Is't not your Aunts desire too?

NIECE
What a dissembling croane's that! she'l forswear't now.

CUNNINGAME
I see my project takes, yonder's the grace on't.

NIECE
Who would put confidence in wit again,
I'm plagu'd for my ambition, to desire
A wise Man for a husband, and I see
Fate will not have us go beyond our stint,
We are allow'd but one dish, and that's Woodcock,
It keeps up wit to make us friends and servants of,
And thinks any thing's good enough to make us husbands;
Oh that Whores hat o' thine, o' the riding block,
A shade for lecherous kisses.

CUNNINGAME
Make you doubt on't?
Is not my love of force?

NIECE
Yes, me it forces
To tear that sorcerous strumpet from th' imbraces.

CUNNINGAME
Lady?

NIECE
Oh thou hast wrong'd the exquisit'st love—

CUNNINGAME
What mean you, Lady?

NIECE
Mine, you'l answer for't.

CUNNINGAME
Alas, What seek you?

NIECE
Sir, mine own with loss.

CUNNINGAME
You shall.

NIECE
I never made so hard a bargain.

CUNNINGAME
Sweet Lady?

NIECE
Unjust man, let my wrath reach her,
As you owe virtue duty;

[**CUNNINGAME** falls on purpose.

Your cause trips you,
Now Minion, you shall feel what loves rage is,
Before you taste the pleasure; smile you false, Sir?

CUNNINGAME
How can I chuse? to see what pains you take,
Upon a thing will never thank you for't.

NIECE
How?

CUNNINGAME
See what things you women be, Lady,
When cloaths are taken for the best part of you?
This was to show you, when you think I love you not,
How y'are deceiv'd still, there the Moral lies,
'Twas a trap set to catch you, and the only bait
To take a Lady nibling, is fine clothes;
Now I dare boldly thank you for your love,
I'm pretty well resolv'd in't by this fit,
For a jealous ague alwayes ushers it.

NIECE

Now blessings still maintain this wit of thine,
And I have an excellent fortune coming in thee,
Bring nothing else I charge thee.

CUNNINGAME
Not a groat I warrant ye.

NIECE
Thou shalt be worthily welcome, take my faith for't,
Next opportunity shall make us.

CUNNINGAME
The old Gentlewoman has fool'd her revenge sweetly.

NIECE
'Lass, 'tis her part, she knows her place so well yonder;
Alwayes when Women jumpe upon threescore,
Love shoves e'm from the chamber to the door.

CUNNINGAME
Thou art a precious she-wit.

[Exeunt.

ACTUS QUINTUS

SCÆNA PRIMA

Enter **CUNNINGHAME**, at one door, **WITTY-PATE**, **SIR RUINOUS**, **LADY RUINOUS**, and **PRISCIAN** at the other.

CUNNINGAME
Friend, met in the harvest of our designs,
Not a thought but's busie.

WITTY-PATE
I knew it Man,
And that made me provide these needful Reapers,
Hooks, Rakers, Gleaners; we'll sing it home
With a melodious Horne-pipe; this is the Bond,
That as we further in your great affair,
You'l suffer us to glean, pick up for crums,
And if we snatch a handful from the sheaf,
You will not look a churle on's.

CUNNINGAME

Friend, we'll share
The sheaves of gold, only the Love Aker
Shall be peculiar.

WITTY-PATE
Much good do you, Sir,
Away, you know your way, and your stay; get you
The Musick ready, while we prepare the dancers.

SIR RUINOUS
We are a consort of our selves.

PRISCIAN
And can strike up lustily.

WITTY-PATE
You must bring Sir Fop.

CUNNINGAME
That's perfect enough.

SIR RUINOUS
Bring all the Fops you can, the more, the better fare
So the proverb runs backwards.

[Exeunt **SIR RUINOUS** and **PRISCIAN**.

LADY RUINOUS
I'll bring the Ladies.

[Exit.

WITTY-PATE
Do so first, and then the Fops will follow;
I must to my Father, he must make one.

[Exit.

[Enter **TWO SERVANTS** with a Banquet.

CUNNINGAME
While I dispatch a business with the Knight,
And I go with you. Well sed, I thank you,
This small Banquet will furnish our few Guests
With taste and state enough; one reach my Gown.
The action craves it rather than the weather.

1ST SERVANT

There's one stayes to speak with you, Sir.

CUNNINGAME
What is he?

1ST SERVANT
Faith I know not what, Sir, a Fool, I think,
That some Brokers shop has made half a Gentleman;
Has the name of a Worthy too.

CUNNINGAME
Pompey? Is't not?

1ST SERVANT
That's he, Sir.

CUNNINGAME
Alas, poor fellow, prethee enter him, he will need too.

[Enter **SECOND SERVANT** with a Gown.

He shall serve for a Witness. Oh Gramercy:
If my friend Sir Gregory comes, you know him,

[Enter **CLOWN**.

Entertain him kindly.
Oh Master Pompey, How is't man?

CLOWN
'Snails, I'm almost starv'd with Love, and cold, and one thing or other;
Has not my Lady sent for me yet?

CUNNINGAME
Not that I hear, sure some unfriendly Messenger
Is imploy'd betwixt you.

CLOWN
I was ne'er so cold in my life, in my Conscience I have been seven mile in length, along the New River; I have seen a hundred stickle bags; I do not think but there's gudgeons too; 'twill ne'er be a true water.

CUNNINGAME
Why think you so?

CLOWN
I warrant you, I told a thousand Millers thumbs in it,
I'll make a little bold with your Sweet-meats.

CUNNINGAME
And welcome Pompey.

CLOWN
'Tis a strange thing, I have no taste in any thing.

CUNNINGAME
Oh, that's Love, that distasts any thing but it self.

CLOWN
'Tis worse than Cheese in that point, may not a Man break his word with a Lady? I could find in my heart and my hose too.

CUNNINGAME
By no means, Sir, that breaks all the Laws of Love.

CLOWN
Well, I'll ne'er pass my word without my deed to
A Lady, while I live agen, I would fain recover my taste.

CUNNINGAME
Well, I have news to tell you.

CLOWN
Good news, Sir?

CUNNINGAME
Happy news, I help you away with a Rival your Master bestow'd.

CLOWN
Where, for this Plumbs sake—

CUNNINGAME
Nay, listen me.

CLOWN
I warrant you, Sir, I have two ears to one mouth,
I hear more than I eat, I'de ne'er row by Queen Hive
While I liv'd else.

CUNNINGAME
I have a Wife for him, and thou shalt witness the Contract.

CLOWN
The old one I hope, 'tis not the Lady?

CUNNINGAME
Choak him first, 'tis one which thou shalt see,

See him, see him deceiv'd, see the deceit, only
The injunction is, you shall smile with modesty.

CLOWN
I'll simper I'faith, as cold as I am yet, the old one
I hope.

[Enter **SERVANT**.

SERVANT
Sir, here's Sir Gregory.

CUNNINGAME
U'd so, shelter, shelter, if you be seen,
All's ravell'd out again; stand there private,
And you'll find the very opportunity
To call you forth, and place you at the Table.

[Enter **SIR GREGORY**.

You are welcome, Sir, this Banquet will serve,
When it is crown'd with such a dainty as you
Expect, and must have.

SIR GREGORY
'Tush, these sweet-meats are but sauce to that,
Well, if there be any honesty, or true word in a dream,
She's mine own, nay, and chang'd extreamly,
Not the same Woman.

CUNNINGAME
Who, not the Lady?

SIR GREGORY
No, not to me, the edge of her tongue is taken off,
Gives me very good words, turn'd up-side-down to me,
And we live as quietly as two Tortoises, if she hold on,
As she began in my dream.

[Soft Musick.

CUNNINGAME
Nay, if Love send forth such Predictions,
You are bound to believe 'em, there's the watch-word
Of her coming; to your practis'd part now,
If you hit it, Æquus Cupido nobis.

[Both go into the Gown.

SIR GREGORY
I will warrant you, Sir, I will give armes to
Your Gentry, look you forward to your business,
I am an eye behind you, place her in that Chair,
And let me alone to grope her out.

[Enter **MIRABELL**.

CUNNINGAME
Silence, Lady, your sweet presence illustrates
This homely roof, and, as course entertainment;
But where affections are both Host and Guest,
They cannot meet unkindly; please you sit,
Your something long stay made me unmannerly,
To place before you, you know this friend here,
He's my Guest, and more especially,
That this our meeting might not be too single,
Without a witness to't.

MIRABELL
I came not unresolv'd, Sir,
And when our hands are clasp'd in that firm faith
Which I expect from you; fame shall be bold
To speak the loudest on't: oh you grasp me
Somewhat too hard friend.

CUNNINGAME
That's Love's eager will,
I'll touch it gentlier.

[Kisses her hand.

MIRABELL
That's too low in you,
Less it be doubly recompenc'd in me.

[She kisses his hand.

CLOWN
Puh, I must stop my mouth, I shall be choakt else.

CUNNINGAME
Come, we'll not play and trifle with delayes,
We met to joyn these hands, and willingly
I cannot leave it till confirmation.

MIRABELL

One word first, how does your friend, kind Sir Gregory?

CUNNINGAME
Why do you mention him? you love him not?

MIRABELL
I shall love you the less if you say so, Sir,
In troth I love him, but 'tis you deceive him,
This flattering hand of yours does rob him now,
Now you steal his right from him, and I know
I shall have hate for't, his hate extreamly.

CUNNINGAME
Why I thought you had not come so weakly arm'd,
Upon my life the Knight will love you for't,
Exceedingly love you, for ever love you.

MIRABELL
I, you'll perswade me so.

CUNNINGAME
Why he's my friend,
And wishes me a fortune equal with him,
I know, and dare speak it for him.

MIRABELL
Oh, this hand betrayes him, you might remember him in some courtesie yet at least.

CUNNINGAME
I thank your help in't, here's to his health
Where e'er he be.

MIRABELL
I'll pledge it, were it against my health.

CLOWN
Oh, oh, my heart hops after twelve mile a day, upon a good return, now could I walk three hundred mile a foot, and laugh forwards and backwards.

MIRABELL
You'll take the Knights health, Sir.

CLOWN
Yes, yes forsooth, oh my sides! such a Banquet once a week, would make me grow fat in a fortnight.

CUNNINGAME
Well, now to close our meeting, with the close
Of mutual hands and hearts, thus I begin,

Here in Heavens eye, and all loves sacred powers,
(Which in my Prayers stand propitious)
I knit this holy hand fast, and with this hand
The heart that owes this hand, ever binding
By force of this initiating Contract
Both heart and hand in love, faith, loyalty,
Estate, or what to them belongs, in all the dues,
Rights and honors of a faithful husband,
And this firm vow, henceforth till death, to stand
Irrevocable, seal'd both with heart and hand.

MIRABELL
Which thus I second, but oh, Sir Gregory.

CUNNINGAME
Agen? this interposition's ill, believe me.

MIRABELL
Here, in Heavens eye, and all Loves sacred powers,
I knit this holy hand fast, and with this hand
The heart that owes this hand, ever binding
Both heart and hand in love, honor, loyalty,
Estate, or what to them belongs in all the dues,
Rights, and duties of a true faithful Wife;
And this firm Vow, henceforth till death, to stand,
Irrevocable, seal'd both with heart and hand.

SIR GREGORY
A full agreement on both parts.

CUNNINGAME
I, here's witness of that.

SIR GREGORY
Nay, I have over-reacht you Lady, and that's much,
For any Knight in England to over-reach a Lady.

MIRABELL
I rejoyce in my deceit, I am a Lady
Now, I thank you, Sir.

CLOWN
Good morrow Lady Fop.

SIR GREGORY
'Snails, I'm gull'd, made a worshipful ass, this is not my Lady.

CUNNINGAME

But it is Sir, and true as your dream told you,
That your Lady was become another Woman.

SIR GREGORY
I'll have another Lady, Sir, if there were no more
Ladies in London, blind-man buff is an unlawful Game.

CUNNINGAME
Come, down on your knees first, and thank your Stars.

SIR GREGORY
A fire of my stars, I may thank you, I think.

CUNNINGAME
So you may pray for me, and honor me,
That have preserv'd you from a lasting torment,
For a perpetual comfort; Did you call me friend?

SIR GREGORY
I pray pardon me for that, I did miscall you, I confess.

CUNNINGAME
And should I, receiving such a thankful name,
Abuse it in the act? Should I see my friend
Bafled, disgrac'd, without any reverence
To your title, to be call'd slave, rascal?
Nay curst to your face, fool'd, scorn'd, beaten down
With a womans peevish hate, yet I should stand
And suffer you to be lost, cast away?
I would have seen you buried quick first,
Your spurs of Knighthood to have wanted rowels,
And to be kickt from your heels; slave, rascall?
Hear this Tongue?

MIRABELL
My dearest Love, sweet Knight, my Lord, my Husband.

CUNNINGAME
So, this is not slave, and rascall then.

MIRABELL
What shall your eye command, but shall be done,
In all the duties of a loyal Wife?

CUNNINGAME
Good, good, are not curses fitter for you? wer't not better
Your head were broke with the handle of a fan,
Or your nose bor'd with a silver bodkin?

MIRABELL

Why, I will be a servant in your Lady.

CUNNINGAME

'Pox, but you shall not, she's too good for you,
This contract shall be a nullity, I'll break't off,
And see you better bestow'd.

SIR GREGORY

'Slid, but you shall not, Sir, she's mine own, and I am hers, and we are one anothers lawfully, and let me
see him that will take her away by the Civil Law: if you be my friend, keep you so, if you have done me a
good turn, do not hit me i'th' teeth with't, that's not the part of a friend.

CUNNINGAME

If you be content—

SIR GREGORY

Content? I was never in better contention in my life.
I'll not change her for both the Exchanges, New or the Old;
Come, kiss me boldly.

CLOWN

Give you joy, Sir.

SIR GREGORY

Oh Sir, I thank you as much as though I did, you are belov'd of Ladies, you see we are glad of under-
women.

CLOWN

Ladies? let not Ladies be disgrac'd, you are as it were a Married Man, and have a family, and for the
parties sake that was unnam'd before, being Pese-cod time, I am appeas'd, yet I would wish you make a
Ruler of your Tongue.

CUNNINGAME

Nay, no dissention here, I must bar that,
And this (friend) I entreat you, and be advis'd,
Let this private contract be yet conceal'd,
And still support a seeming face of love
Unto the Lady; mark how it availes you,
And quits all her scorns, her Unckle is now hot
In pursuit of the match, and will enforce her,
Bend her proud stomach, that she shall proffer
Her self to you, which when you have flouted,
And laught your fill at, you shall scorn her off,
With all your disgraces trebled upon her,
For there the pride of all her heart will bow,
When you shall foot her from you, not she you.

SIR GREGORY
Good I'faith; I'll continue it, I'd fain laugh at the old fellow too, for he has abus'd me as scurvily as his Neece, my Knight-hood's upon the spur, we'll go to Bed, and then to Church as fast as we can.

[Exit **SIR GREGORY** and **MIRABELL**.

CLOWN
I do wonder I do not hear of the Lady yet.

CUNNINGAME
The good minute may come sooner than you are aware of, I do not think but 'twill e'r night yet, as near as 'tis.

CLOWN
Well, I will go walk by the New River, in that meditation, I am o'er shooes, I'm sure upon the drie bank, this gullery of my Master will keep me company this two hours too, if love were not an enemy to laughter, I should drive away the time well enough; you know my walk, Sir, if she sends, I shall be found angling, for I will try what I can catch for luck sake, I will fish fair for't,
Oh Knight, that thou shouldst be gull'd so; ha, ha, it does me good at heart,
But oh Lady, thou tak'st down my merry part.

[Exit.

[Enter **WITTY-PATE**.

WITTY-PATE
Friend.

CUNNINGAME
Here friend.

WITTY-PATE
All's afoot, and will goe smooth away,
The woman has conquer'd the women, they are gone,
Which I have already complain'd to my Father,
Suggesting that Sir Gregory is fall'n off
From his charge, for neglects and ill usage,
And that he is most violently bent
On Gentries wife (whom I have call'd a widow)
And that without most sudden prevention
He will be married to her.

CUNNINGAME
Fool, all this is wrong,
This wings his pursuit, and will be before me; I am lost for ever.

WITTY-PATE

No, stay, you shall not go
But with my Father, on my wit let it lie,
You shall appear a friendly assistant,
To help in all affairs, and in execution
Help your self only.

CUNNINGAME
Would my belief
Were strong in this assurance.

WITTY-PATE
You shall credit it,
And my wit shall be your slave, if it deceive you.

[Enter **SIR PERFIDIOUS**.

My Father—

SIR PERIFIDIOUS
Oh Sir, you are well met, where's the Knight your friend?

CUNNINGAME
Sir, I think your Son has told you.

WITTY-PATE
Shall I stand to tell't agen? I tell you he loves,
But not my Kinswoman, her base usage,
And your slack performance which he accuses most
Indeed, has turn'd the Knights heart upside down.

SIR PERIFIDIOUS
I'll curb her for't, can he be but recover'd,
He shall have her, and she shall be dutiful,
And love him as a Wife too.

WITTY-PATE
With that condition, Sir,
I dare recall him were he enter'd the Church,
So much interest of love I assure in him.

SIR PERIFIDIOUS
Sir, it shall be no loss to you if you do.

WITTY-PATE
I, but these are words still, will not the deeds
Be wanting at the recovery, if it should be agen?

SIR PERFIDIOUS

Why here fool, I am provided, five hunder'd in earnest,
Of the thousands in her Dower, but were they married once,
I'd cut him short enough, that's my agreement.

WITTY-PATE
I, now I perceive some purpose in you, Father.

SIR PERIFIDIOUS
But wherefore is she then stol'n out of doors to him?

WITTY-PATE
To him? oh fie upon your error, she has another
object, believe it, Sir.

SIR PERIFIDIOUS
I never could perceive it.

CUNNINGAME
I did Sir, and to her shame I should speak it,
To my own sorrow I saw it, dalliance,
Nay, dotage with a very Clown, a Fool.

SIR PERIFIDIOUS
Wit and wantons? nothing else? nothing else?
She love a fool? she'll sooner make a Fool
Of a wise man.

CUNNINGAME
I, my friend complains so,
Sir Gregory says flatly, she makes a fool of him,
And these bold circumstances are approv'd:
Favours have been sent by him, yet he ignorant
Whither to carry 'em; they have been understood,
And taken from him, certain, Sir, there is
An unsuspected fellow lies conceal'd,
What, or where e'er he is, these slight neglects
Could not be of a Knight else.

SIR PERIFIDIOUS
Well Sir, you have promis'd (if we recover him
Unmarried) to salve all these old bruises?

CUNNINGAME
I'll do my best, Sir.

SIR PERIFIDIOUS
I shall thank you, costly Sir, and kindly too.

WITTY-PATE

Will you talk away the time here, Sir, and come
behind all your purposes?

SIR PERIFIDIOUS

Away good Sir.

WITTY-PATE

Then stay a little, good Sir, for my advice,
Why, Father are you broke? your wit beggar'd,
Or are you at your wits end? or out of
Love with wit? no trick of wit to surprize
Those designs, but with open Hue and Cry,
For all the world to talk on, this is strange,
You were not wont to slubber a project so.

SIR PERIFIDIOUS

Can you help at a pinch now? shew your self
My Son, go too, I leave this to your wit,
Because I'll make a proof on't.

WITTY-PATE

'Tis thus then,
I have had late intelligence, they are now
Bucksom as Bacchus Froes, revelling, dancing,
Telling the Musicks numbers with their feet,
Awaiting the meeting of premonish'd friends,
That's questionless, little dreading you,
Now Sir, with a dexterous trick indeed, suddain
And sufficient were well, to enter on um
As something like the abstract of a Masque;
What though few persons? if best for our purpose
That commends the project.

SIR PERIFIDIOUS

This takes up time.

WITTY-PATE

Not at all, I can presently furnish
With loose disguises that shall fit that Scene.

SIR PERIFIDIOUS

Why what wants then?

WITTY-PATE

Nothing but charge of Musick,
That must be paid, you know.

SIR PERIFIDIOUS
That shall be my charges, I'll pay the Musick.
What e'er it cost.

WITTY-PATE
And that shall be all your charge,
Now on, I like it, there will be wit in't Father.

[Exit **SIR PERIFIDIOUS** and **WITTY-PATE**.

CUNNINGAME
I will neither distrust his wit nor friendship,
Yet if his Master brain should be o'er-thrown
My resolution now shall seize mine own.

[Exit.

[Enter **NIECE**, **LADY RUINOUS**, **GUARDIANESS**, **SIR RUINOUS**, **PRISCIAN**, with instruments masqu'd.

LADY RUINOUS
Nay, let's have Musick, let that sweet breath at least
Give us her airy welcome, 'twill be the best
I fear this ruin'd receptacle will yield,
But that most freely.

NIECE
My welcome follows me,
Else I am ill, come hither, you assure me
Still Mr. Cunningame will be here, and that it was
His kind entreaty that wish'd me meet him.

LADY RUINOUS
Else let me be that shame unto my Sex,
That all belief may flie um.

NIECE
Continue still
The Knights name unto my Guardianess,
She expects no other.

LADY RUINOUS
He will, he will, assure you
Lady, Sir Gregory will be here, and suddainly
This Musick fore-ran him, is't not so consorts?

SIR RUINOUS
Yes Lady, he stays on some device to bring along
Such a labour he was busie in, some witty device.

NIECE

'Twill be long e'r he comes then, for wits a great
Labour to him.

GUARDIANESS

Well, well, you'll agree better one day.

NIECE

Scarce two I think.

GUARDIANESS

Such a mock-beggar suit of cloaths as led me
Into the fools pair-of-Dice, with Dewze Ace,
He that would make me Mistriss Cun, Cun, Cunnie,
He's quite out of my mind, but I shall ne'er
Forget him, while I have a hole in my head;
Such a one I think would please you better,
Though he did abuse you.

SIR RUINOUS

Fye, speak well of him now,
Your Neece has quitted him.

GUARDIANESS

I hope she has,
Else she loses me for ever; but for Sir Gregory.
Would he were come, I shall ill answer this
Unto your Uncle else.

NIECE

You know 'tis his pleasure
I should keep him company.

GUARDIANESS

I, and should be your own
If you did well too: Lord, I do wonder
At the niceness of you Ladies now a days,
They must have Husbands with so much wit forsooth.
Worship and wealth were both wont to be
In better request I'm sure, I cannot tell,
But they get ne'er the wiser children that I see.

LADY RUINOUS

La, la, la, la, Sol, this Musick breaths in vain;
Methinks 'tis dull to let it move alone,
Let's have a female motion, 'tis in private,
And we'll grace't our selves, however it deserves.

NIECE
What say you Guardianess?

GUARDIANESS
'Las I'm weary with the walk,
My jaunting days are done.

LADY RUINOUS
Come, come, we'll fetch her in by course, or else
She shall pay the Musick.

GUARDIANESS
Nay, I'll have a little for my money then.

[They Dance, a Cornet is winded.

LADY RUINOUS
Hark! upon my life the Knight; 'tis your friend,
This was the warning-piece of his approach.

[Enter **SIR PERFIDIOUS, WITTY-PATE, CUNNINGAME**, Masqu'd, and take them to Dance.

LADY RUINOUS
Ha? no words but mum? well then,
We shall need no counsel-keeping.

NIECE
Cunningame?

CUNNINGAME
Yes, fear nothing.

NIECE
Fear? why do you tell me of it?

CUNNINGAME
Your Uncles here.

NIECE
Aye me.

CUNNINGAME
Peace.

SIR PERIFIDIOUS
We have caught 'em.

WITTY-PATE
Thank my wit Father.

GUARDIANESS
Which is the Knight think you?

NIECE
I know not, he will be found when he speaks,
No Masque can disguise his tongue.

WITTY-PATE
Are you charg'd?

SIR PERIFIDIOUS
Are you awake?

WITTY-PATE
I'm answer'd in a question.

CUNNINGAME
Next change we meet, we lose our hands no more.

NIECE
Are you prepar'd to tye 'em?

CUNNINGAME
Yes,
You must go with me.

GUARDIANESS
Whither Sir? not from my charge believe me.

CUNNINGAME
She goes along.

NIECE
Will you venture and my Uncle here?

CUNNINGAME
His stay's prepar'd for.

GUARDIANESS
'Tis the Knight sure, I'll follow.

[Exit **CUNNINGAME**, **NIECE** and **GUARDIANESS**.

SIR PERIFIDIOUS
How now, the Musick tir'd before us?

SIR RUINOUS
Yes Sir, we must be paid now.

WITTY-PATE
Oh that's my charge, Father.

SIR PERIFIDIOUS
But stay, where are our wanton Ladies gone?
Son, where are they?

WITTY-PATE
Only chang'd the room in a change, that's all sure.

SIR PERIFIDIOUS
I'll make 'em all sure else, and then return to you.

SIR RUINOUS
You must pay for your Musick first, Sir.

SIR PERIFIDIOUS
Must? are there musty Fidlers? are Beggars choosers now?
Ha! why Witty-pate, Son, where am I?

WITTY-PATE
You were dancing e'en now, in good measure, Sir,
Is your health miscarried since? what ail you, Sir?

SIR PERIFIDIOUS
Death, I may be gull'd to my face, where's my Neece?
What are you?

LADY RUINOUS
None of your Neece, Sir.

SIR PERIFIDIOUS
How now? have you loud instruments too? I'll hear
No more, I thank you; what have I done to
To bring these fears about me? Son, where am I?

WITTY-PATE
Not where you should be, Sir, you should be paying
For your Musick, and you are in a maze.

SIR PERIFIDIOUS
Oh, is't so, put up, put up, I pray you,
Here's a crown for you.

LADY RUINOUS
Pish, a crown?

SIR RUINOUS & **PRISCIAN**
Ha, ha, ha, a crown?

SIR PERIFIDIOUS
Which way do you laugh? I have seen a crown
Has made a Consort laugh heartily.

WITTY-PATE
Father,
To tell you truth, these are no ordinary
Musicians, they expect a bounty
Above their punctual desert.

SIR PERIFIDIOUS
A pox on your Punks, and their deserts too.
Am I not cheated all this while think you?
Is not your pate in this?

WITTY-PATE
If you be cheated,
You are not to be indicted for your own goods,
Here you trifle time to market your bounty
And make it base, when it must needs be free
For ought I can perceive.

SIR PERIFIDIOUS
Will you know the lowest price, Sir?

WITTY-PATE
That I will Sir, with all my heart.

SIR PERIFIDIOUS
Unless I was discover'd, and they now fled
Home agen for fear, I am absolutely beguil'd,
That's the best can be hop'd for.

WITTY-PATE
Faith 'tis somewhat too dear yet, Gentlemen.

SIR RUINOUS
There's not a Denier to be bated, Sir.

SIR PERIFIDIOUS
Now Sir, how dear is it?

WITTY-PATE
Bate but the t'other ten pound?

PRISCIAN
Not a Bawbee, Sir.

SIR PERIFIDIOUS
How? bate ten pound? what's the whole sum then?

WITTY-PATE
Faith Sir, a hundred pound, with much adoe,
I got fifty bated, and faith Father, to say truth,
'Tis reasonable for men of their fashion.

SIR PERIFIDIOUS
La, la, la, down, a hunder'd pound? la, la, la,
You are a Consort of Thieves, are you not?

WITTY-PATE
No Musicians, Sir, I told you before.

SIR PERIFIDIOUS
Fiddle faddle, is it not a robbery? a plain robbery.

WITTY-PATE
No, no, no, by no means Father, you have receiv'd
For your money, nay and that you cannot give back,
'Tis somewhat dear I confess, but who can help it?
If they had been agreed with before-hand,
'Twas ill forgotten.

SIR PERFIDIOUS
And how many shares have you in this? I see my force,
Case up your instruments, I yield, here, as robb'd and
Taken from me, I deliver it.

WITTY-PATE
No Sir, you have perform'd your promise now,
Which was, to pay the charge of Musick, that's all.

SIR PERIFIDIOUS
I have heard no Musick, I have receiv'd none, Sir,
There's none to be found in me, nor about me.

WITTY-PATE
Why Sir, here's witness against you, you have danc'd,
And he that dances, acknowledges a receipt of Musick.

SIR PERIFIDIOUS
I denie that, Sir, look you, I can dance without Musick, do you see, Sir? and I can sing without it too; you are a Consort of Thieves, do you hear what I do?

WITTY-PATE
Pray you take heed, Sir, if you do move the
Musick agen, it may cost you as much more.

SIR PERIFIDIOUS
Hold, hold, I'll depart quietly, I need not bid you farewel, I think now, so long as that hundred pound lasts with you.

[Enter **GUARDIANESS**.

Ha, ha, am I snapt i'faith?

GUARDIANESS
Oh, Sir, Perfidious.

SIR PERIFIDIOUS
I, I, some howling another while, Musick's too damnable dear.

GUARDIANESS
Oh Sir, my heart-strings are broke, if I can but live to tell you the tale, I care not, your Neece my charge is—

SIR PERIFIDIOUS
What, is she sick?

GUARDIANESS
No, no Sir, she's lustily well married.

SIR PERIFIDIOUS
To whom?

GUARDIANESS
Oh, to that cunning dissembler, Cunningame.

SIR PERIFIDIOUS
I'll hang the Priest, first, what was he?

GUARDIANESS
Your kinsman, Sir, that has the Welch Benefice.

SIR PERIFIDIOUS
I sav'd him from the Gallows to that end, good: is there any more?

GUARDIANESS

And Sir Gregory is married too.

SIR PERIFIDIOUS
To my Neece too, I hope, and then I may hang her.

GUARDIANESS
No Sir, to my Neece, thank Cupid; and that's all that's likely to recover me, she's Lady Fop now, and I am One of her Aunts, I thank my promotion.

[Enter **CREDULOUS, CUNNINGAME, NIECE, SIR GREGORY,** and **MIRABELL.**

CREDULOUS
I have perform'd your behest, Sir.

SIR PERIFIDIOUS
What have you perform'd, Sir?

WITTY-PATE
Faith Sir I must excuse my Cosin in this act,
If you can excuse your self for making him
A Priest, there's the most difficult answer.
I put this practise on him, as from your desire,
A truth, a truth, Father.

CREDULOUS
I protest, Sir, he tells you truth, he mov'd me to't in your name.

SIR PERIFIDIOUS
I protest, Sir, he told you a lye in my name, and were you so easie, Mr. Credulous, to believe him?

CREDULOUS
If a man should not believe his Cosin, Sir, whom should he believe?

SIR PERIFIDIOUS
Good'en to you, good Mr. Cosin Cunningame,
And your fair Bride, my Cosin Cunningame too,
And how do you Sir Gregory, with your fair Lady?

SIR GREGORY
A little better than you would have had me, I thank you Sir, the days of Puppy, and Slave, and Rascal, are pretty well blown over now, I know Crabs from Verjuyce, I have tried both, and thou'dst give me thy Neece for nothing, I'd not have her.

CUNNINGAME
I think so Sir Gregory, for my sake you would not.

SIR GREGORY

I wou'd thou hadst scap'd her too, and then she had died of the Green sickness: know this, that I did marry in spight, and I will kiss my Lady in spight, and love her in spight, and beget children of her in spight, and when I dye, they shall have my Lands in spight; this was my resolution, and now 'tis out.

NIECE
How spightful are you now, Sir Gregory!
Why look you, I can love my dearest Husband,
With all the honors, duties, sweet embraces,
That can be thrown upon a loving man.

SIR GREGORY
This is afore your Uncles face, but behind his back, in private, you'll shew him another tale—

CUNNINGAME
You see, Sir, now the irrecoverable state of all these things before you: come out of your muse, they have been but Wit-weapons, you were wont to love the Play.

[Enter **CLOWN**.

SIR PERIFIDIOUS
Let me alone in my muse a little, Sir, I will wake to you anon.

CUNNINGAME
U'd so, your friend Pompey, how will you answer him?

NIECE
Very well, if you'll but second it, and help me.

CLOWN
I do hear strange stories, are Ladies things obnoxious?

NIECE
Oh, the dissembling falsest wretch is come.

CUNNINGAME
How now Lady?

NIECE
Let me come to him, and instead of love
Let me have revenge.

WITTY-PATE
Pray you now, will you first examine, whether he
be guilty or no.

NIECE
He cannot be excus'd,
How many Messengers (thou perjur'd man)

Hast thou return'd with Vows and Oaths, that thou
Wouldst follow, and never till this unhappy hour
Could I set eye of thee, since thy false eye
Drew my heart to it? oh I could tear thee now,
Instead of soft embraces, pray give me leave—

WITTY-PATE
Faith this was ill done of you Sir, if you promis'd otherwise.

CLOWN
By this hand, never any Messenger came at me, since the first time I came into her company; that a man should be wrong'd thus!

NIECE
Did not I send thee Scarfs and Diamonds?
And thou return'dst me Letters, one with a false heart in't.

WITTY-PATE
Oh fie, to receive favours, return falshoods, and hold a Lady in hand—

CLOWN
Will you believe me, Sir? if ever I receiv'd Diamonds,
or Scarf, or sent any Letter to her, would this sword might
ne'er go through me.

WITTY-PATE
Some bad Messengers have gone between you then.

NIECE
Take him from my sight if I shall see to morrow.

WITTY-PATE
Pray you forbear the place, this discontent may impair
her health much.

CLOWN
'Foot, if a man had been in any fault, 'twould ne'er a
griev'd him, Sir, if you'll believe.

WITTY-PATE
Nay, nay, protest no more, I do believe you,
But you see how the Lady is wrong'd by't;
She has cast away her self, it is to be fear'd,
Against her Uncles Will, nay, any consent,
But out of a mere neglect, and spight to her self,
Married suddainly without any advice.

CLOWN

Why, who can help it? if she be cast away, she may thank her self, she might have gone farther and far'd worse; I could do no more than I could do: 'twas her own pleasure to command me, that I should not come, till I was sent for, I had been with her every minute of an hour else.

WITTY-PATE
Truly I believe you.

CLOWN
Night and day she might have commanded me, and that she knew well enough; I said as much to her between her and I; yet I protest, she's as honest a Lady for my part, that I'd say, if she would see me hang'd: if she be cast away I cannot help it, she might have stay'd to have spoke with a man.

WITTY-PATE
Well, 'twas a hard miss on both parts.

CLOWN
So 'twas, I was within one of her, for all this cross luck, I was sure I was between the Knight and home.

NIECE
Not gone yet? oh my heart! none regard my health?

WITTY-PATE
Good Sir, forbear her sight awhile, you hear how ill she brooks it.

CLOWN
Foolish woman, to overthrow her fortunes so; I shall think the worse of a Ladies wit, while I live for't—I could almost cry for anger, if she should miscarry now; 'twould touch my conscience a little, and who knows what love and conceit may do? what would people say, as I go along? there goes he that the Lady died for love on, I am sure to hear on't i'th' streets, I shall weep before hand; foolish woman, I do grieve more for thee now, than I did love thee before; well, go thy ways, wouldst thou spare thy Husbands head, and break thine own heart? if thou hadst any wit, I would some other had been the cause of thy undoing, I shall be twitted i'th' teeth with it, I'm sure of that, foolish Lady.

[Exit.

NIECE
So, so, this trouble's well shook off, Uncle, how d'ye? there's a Dowrie due, Sir.

CUNNINGAME
We have agreed it sweetest,
And find your Uncle fully recover'd, kind to both of us.

WITTY-PATE
To all the rest I hope.

SIR PERIFIDIOUS
Never to thee, nor thee, easie cosin Credulous,
Was your wit so raw?

CREDULOUS

Faith yours Sir, so long season'd
Has been faulty too, and very much to blame,
Speaking it with reverence, Uncle.

SIR GREGORY

Yes faith, Sir, you have paid as dear for your time, as any man here.

WITTY-PATE

I Sir, and I'll reckon it to him. Imprimis, The first preface cheat of a pair of pieces to the Beggars, you remember that I was the example to your bounty there, I spake Greek and Syriack, Sir, you understand me now. Next, the Robbery put upon your indulgent Cosin, which indeed was no Robbery, no Constable, no Justice, no Thief, but all Cheaters; there was a hunder'd Mark, mark you that: Lastly, this memorable 100 pounds worth of Musick, this was but cheats and wit too, and for the assistance of this Gentleman to my Cosin (for which I am to have a Fee) that was a little practice of my wit too, Father; will you come to composition yet, Father?

CUNNINGAME

Yes faith Sir, do, two hundr'd a year will be easier than so much weekly, I do not think he's barren if he should be put to't agen.

SIR PERIFIDIOUS

Why this was the day I look'd for, thou shalt have't,
And the next cheat makes it up three hundr'd;
Live thou upon thy ten pound Vicarage,
Thou get'st not a penny more, here's thy full
Hire now.

CREDULOUS

I thank you, Sir.

WITTY-PATE

Why there was the sum of all my Wit, Father,
To shuve him out of your favour, which I fear'd
Would have disinherited me.

SIR PERIFIDIOUS

Most certain it had,
Had not thy wit recover'd it; is there any here
That had a hand with thee?

WITTY-PATE

Yes, all these, Sir.

SIR PERIFIDIOUS

Nephew, part a hundr'd pound amongst 'em,
I'll repay it; wealth, love me as I love wit;

When I die,
I'll build an Alms-house for decay'd wits.

SIR GREGORY
I'll entertain one in my life time; Scholar, you shall be my Chaplain, I have the gift of twenty Benefices,
simple as I am here.

PRISCIAN
Thanks my great Patron.

CUNNINGAME
Sir your Gentry and your name shall both be rais'd as high as my fortunes can reach 'em, for your friends
sake.

WITTY-PATE
Something will be in my present power, the future more,
You shall share with me.

SIR RUINOUS and **WIFE**
Thanks worthy Gentlemen.

NIECE
Sir, I would beg one thing of you.

SIR GREGORY
You can beg nothing of me.

WITTY-PATE
Oh Sir, if she begs, there's your power over her.

SIR GREGORY
She has begg'd me for a fool already, but 'tis no matter.
I have begg'd her for a Lady, that she might have been,
That's one for another.

WITTY-PATE
Nay, but if she beg—

SIR GREGORY
Let her beg agen then.

NIECE
That your man Pompey's Coat may come over his ears back agen, I would not he should be lost for my
sake.

SIR GREGORY
Well, 'tis granted, for mine own sake.

MIRABELL
I'll intreat it Sir.

SIR GREGORY
Why then 'tis granted for your sake.

SIR PERIFIDIOUS
Come, come, down with all weapons now, 'tis Musick time,
So it be purchas'd at an easie rate;
Some have receiv'd the knocks, some giv'n the hits,
And all concludes in love, there's happy wits.

[Exeunt.

THE EPILOGUE

At the Reviving of the Play

We need not tell you Gallants, that this night
The Wits have jumpt, or that the Scenes hit right
'Twould be but labor lost for to excuse
What Fletcher had to do in: his brisk Muse
Was so Mercurial, that if he but writ
An Act, or two, the whole Play rose up wit.
We'll not appeal unto those Gentlemen
Judge by their Cloaths, if they sit right, nor when
The Ladies smile, and with their Fanns delight
To whisk a clinch aside, then all goes right:
'Twas well receiv'd before, and we dare say,
You now are welcome to no vulgar Play.

Thomas Middleton – A Short Biography

Thomas Middleton was born in London in April 1580 and baptised on 18th April. He was the son of a bricklayer who had raised himself to the status of a gentleman and become the owner of property adjoining the Curtain Theatre in Shoreditch.

Middleton was aged only five when his father died. His mother remarried but this new union unfortunately fell apart and turned into a fifteen year legal conflict centered on the inheritance of Thomas and his younger sister.

Middleton went on to attend Queen's College, Oxford, matriculating in 1598. However he failed to graduate for reasons unknown leaving either in 1600 or 1601. He had by that time written and published three long poems in popular Elizabethan styles. None appears to have been commercially successful although Microcynicon: Six Snarling Satirese was denounced by the Archbishop of Canterbury and publicly burned as part of his attack on verse satire. Although a minor work, the poems show the roots of Middleton's interest in, and later mature work on, sin, hypocrisy, and lust.

In the early years of the 17th century, Middleton made a living writing topical pamphlets, including one, Penniless Parliament of Threadbare Poets, that was reprinted several times as well as becoming the subject of a parliamentary inquiry.

For one so young he was already making quite an impact and had obviously attracted the eye of the authorities in those turbulent times.

Records surviving of the great theatrical entrepreneur of the day, Philip Henslowe, confirm that Middleton was writing for Henslowe's Admiral's Men. His lauded contemporary, a certain William Shakespeare, was writing only for Henslowe whereas Middleton remained a free agent and able to write for whichever theatrical company hired him.

These early years writing plays continued to attract controversy. His friendship and writing partnership with Thomas Dekker brought him into conflict with Ben Jonson and George Chapman in the so-called War of the Theatres. (This controversy was also called the Poetomachia by Thomas Dekker. The Bishops Ban of 1599 had removed any use of satire from prose and verse publications and so the only outlet was on the stage. For the next 3 years Ben Jonson and George Chapman on one side and John Marston, Thomas Dekker and Thomas Middleton on the other poked fun at their opposition with characters from their plays. The grudge against Jonson continued as late as 1626, when Jonson's play The Staple of News indulges in a slur on Middleton's last play, A Game at Chess).

In 1603, Middleton married. It was also a momentous year in other respects. On the death of Elizabeth I, her cousin James VI of Scotland was now also crowned King James I of England. Another outbreak of the plague now forced the theatres in London to close.

For Middleton the changeover from Elizabethan to Jacobean was the beginning of a long period of success as a writer.

When the theatres re-opened and welcomed back audiences in need of entertainment Middleton was there, writing for several different companies. In particular he specialised in city comedy and revenge tragedy.

During this time he appears also to have written with Shakespeare and he is variously attributed as collaborating on All's Well That Ends Well and Timon of Athens.

Although Middleton had started as a junior partner to Thomas Dekker he was now his fully fledged equal. His finest work with Dekker was undoubtedly The Roaring Girl, a biography of the notorious contemporary thief Mary Frith (Frith began her criminal career as a pickpocket before moving on to highway robbery with a penchant for dressing up as a man. A spell in prison was followed by a long career as a 'fence' from her shop in Fleet St. She lived to the then quite extraordinary age of 74.) The writing is noteworthy not only for its playwriting ambition but in producing a fully formed heroine in Moll Cutpurse. This was only shortly after the role of women in plays had seen fit to have them played, in the main, by men.

In the 1610s, Middleton began another playwriting partnership, this time with the actor William Rowley, producing another slew of plays including the classics Wit at Several Weapons and A Fair Quarrel.

The ever adaptable Middleton seemed at ease working with others or by himself. His solo writing credits include the comic masterpiece, A Chaste Maid in Cheapside, in 1613. Interestingly his solo plays are somewhat less thrusting and bellicose. Certainly there is no comedy among them with the satirical depth of Michaelmas Term and no tragedy as raw, striking and as bloodthirsty as The Revenger's Tragedy.

There may be various reasons for this and among them that he was increasingly involved with civic pageants and therefore was trying to avoid too much controversy especially without the cover of a collaborator. Indeed in 1620, he was officially appointed as chronologer of the City of London, a post he held until his death in 1627, when ironically, it passed to his great rival, and sometime enemy, Ben Jonson.

Middleton's official duties did not interrupt his dramatic writing; the 1620s saw the production of his and Rowley's tragedy, and continual favourite, The Changeling, as well as several other tragicomedies.

However in 1624, he reached a peak of notoriety when his dramatic allegory A Game at Chess was staged by the King's Men. The play used the conceit of a chess game to present and satirise the recent intrigues surrounding the Spanish Match; James I's son, Prince Charles, was being positioned to marry the daughter, Maria Anna of the Spanish King Philip IV of Spain. Though Middleton's approach was strongly patriotic, the Privy Council closed the play, after only nine performances at the Globe theatre, having received a complaint from the Spanish ambassador. The Privy Council then opened a prosecution against both authors and actors. Although Middleton in his defence showed that the play had been passed by the Master of the Revels, Sir Henry Herbert, any further performance was forbidden and the author and actors fined.

What happened next is a mystery. It is the last play recorded as having been written by Middleton. His playwriting career appears to have stopped dead. It follows that some sort of further punishment probably occurred and for a writer can there be any greater punishment than not being allowed to write or be heard?

Middleton's work is diverse even by the standards of his age. His career Middleton covers many many genres including tragedy, history and city comedy. As we have noted he did not have the kind of official relationship with a particular company that Shakespeare or Fletcher had that might have supported him in a lean creative period. Instead he appears to have written on a freelance basis for any number of companies. His output ranges from the "snarling" satire of Michaelmas Term, performed by the Children of Paul's, to the bleak intrigues of The Revenger's Tragedy, performed by the King's Men. Interestingly earlier editions of The Revenger's Tragedy attributed the play solely to Cyril Tourneur but recent studies have shredded that view so that Middleton's authorship is not now seriously contested

Indeed modern techniques in analysing writing styles are now leaning towards giving Middleton credit for his adaptation and revision of Shakespeare's Macbeth and Measure for Measure. Along with the more established evidence of collaboration on All's Well That Ends Well and Timon of Athens it appears that Middleton has moved some way forward to the front rank of playwrights and an association, in some form, but its greatest exponent.

His early work was informed by the blossoming, in the late Elizabethan period, of satire, while his maturity was influenced by the ascendancy of Fletcherian tragicomedy. Middleton's later work, in which his satirical fury is tempered and broadened, includes three of his acknowledged masterpieces. A Chaste Maid in Cheapside, produced by the Lady Elizabeth's Men, which skillfully combines London life with an expansive view of the power of love to effect reconciliation even though London seems populated entirely by sinners, in which no social rank goes unsatirised. The Changeling, a later tragedy, returns Middleton to an Italianate setting like that of The Revenger's Tragedy, except that here the central characters are more fully drawn and more compelling as individuals. Similar development can be seen in Women Beware Women.

Middleton's plays are marked by their cynicism, though often very funny, about the human race. His characters are complex. True heroes are a rarity: almost all of his characters are selfish, greedy, and self-absorbed.

When Middleton does portray good people, the characters are often presented as flawless and perfect and given small, undemanding roles. A theological pamphlet attributed to Middleton gives sustenance to the notion that Middleton was a strong believer in Calvinism.

Thomas Middleton died at his home at Newington Butts in Southwark in the summer of 1627, and was buried on July 4th, in St Mary's churchyard which today survives as a public park in Elephant and Castle.

Middleton stands with John Fletcher and Ben Jonson as the most successful and prolific of playwrights from the Jacobean period. Very few Renaissance dramatists would achieve equal success in both comedy and tragedy but Middleton was one. He also wrote many masques and pageants and remains, to this day, one of the most notable of Jacobean dramatists.

Middleton's work has long been praised by many literary critics, among the most fervent were Algernon Charles Swinburne and T. S. Eliot. The latter thought Middleton was second only to Shakespeare.

Among their contemporaries was a very crowded field of talent including: Ben Jonson (1572-1637), Christopher Marlowe (1564-1593), Francis Beaumont (1585-1616), Henry Chettle (1564-1606), John Fletcher (1579–1625), John Ford (1586–1639), John Day (1574-1640), John Marston (1576-1634), John Webster (1580-1634), Nathan Field (1587-1620), Philip Massinger (1584-1640), Richard Burbage (1567-1619), Robert Greene (1558-1592), Thomas Dekker (1575-1625), Thomas Kyd (1558-1594), William Haughton (died 1605), William Rowley (1585-1626).

It's a daunting list and confirms that to top that made you a very special talent indeed.

Thomas Middleton – A Concise Bibliography

It has long been recognised that the modern concept of authorship was rather more elastic in centuries past. Writers were not only for hire, and their work therefore a commodity, but their plays ran much shorter lengths; two weeks being a common term of performance. To that themes and scenes were liberally excised from one play and used in another. Revisions to past plays that were being restaged would be undertaken and entirely credited to other writers. Many works and plays were unpublished and have not survived and some only from memory by actors etc. Whilst many of these playwrights are only now feted for their talents, some undoubtedly were at the time, but it is difficult to, in every case, to establish exact provenance. With modern scholarly and literary techniques author attributions have sometimes changed or been re-balanced. For those where this may be the case we have placed the *Play's Title and other information* in italics

Plays

Blurt, Master Constable or The Spaniard's Night Walk (with Thomas Dekker (1602)

The Phoenix (1603–4)

The Honest Whore, Part 1, a city comedy (1604), (with Thomas Dekker)

Michaelmas Term, a city comedy, (1604)

All's Well That Ends Well (1604-5); believed by some to be co-written by Middleton based on stylometric analysis.

A Trick to Catch the Old One, a city comedy (1605)

A Mad World, My Masters, a city comedy (1605)

A Yorkshire Tragedy, a one-act tragedy (1605); attributed to Shakespeare on its title page, but stylistic analysis favours Middleton.

Timon of Athens a tragedy (1605–6); stylistic analysis indicates that Middleton may have written this play in collaboration with William Shakespeare.

The Puritan (1606)

The Revenger's Tragedy (1606). Earlier editions often mistakenly attribute authorship to Cyril Tourneur.

Your Five Gallants, a city comedy (1607)

The Family of Love (1607) some attribute this to Middleton others include Dekker and Lording Barry.

The Bloody Banquet (1608–9); co-written with Thomas Dekker.

The Roaring Girl, a city comedy depicting the exploits of Mary Frith (1611); with Thomas Dekker.

No Wit, No Help Like a Woman's, a tragic-comedy (1611)

The Second Maiden's Tragedy, a tragedy (1611); an anonymous manuscript; stylistic analysis indicates Middleton's authorship (though one scholar also attributed it to Shakespeare.

A Chaste Maid in Cheapside, a city comedy (1613)

Wit at Several Weapons, a city comedy (1613); printed as part of the Beaumont and Fletcher Folio, but stylistic analysis indicates comprehensive revision by Middleton & Rowley.

More Dissemblers Besides Women, a tragicomedy (1614)

The Widow (1615–16)

The Witch, a tragicomedy (1616)

A Fair Quarrel, a tragicomedy (1616). Co-written with William Rowley.

The Old Law, a tragicomedy (1618–19). written with William Rowley and perhaps a third collaborator.

Hengist, King of Kent, or The Mayor of Quinborough, a tragedy (1620)

Women Beware Women, a tragedy (1621)

Measure for Measure (1603-4); some scholars argue that the First Folio text was partly revised by Middleton in 1621.

Anything for a Quiet Life, a city comedy (1621). Co-written with John Webster.

The Changeling, a tragedy (1622). Co-written with William Rowley.

The Nice Valour (1622). Printed as part of the Beaumont and Fletcher Folio, but stylistic analysis indicates comprehensive revision by Middleton.

The Spanish Gypsy, a tragicomedy (1623). Believed to be a play by Middleton & Rowley and later revised by Thomas Dekker and John Ford.

A Game at Chess, a political satire (1624). Satirized the negotiations over the proposed marriage of Prince Charles, son of James I of England, with the Spanish princess. Closed after nine performances.

Masques & Entertainments

The Whole Royal and Magnificent Entertainment Given to King James Through the City of London (1603–4). Co-written with Thomas Dekker, Stephen Harrison & Ben Jonson.
The Manner of his Lordship's Entertainment
The Triumphs of Truth
Civitas Amor
The Triumphs of Honour and Industry (1617)
The Masque of Heroes, or, The Inner Temple Masque (1619)
The Triumphs of Love and Antiquity (1619)
The World Tossed at Tennis (1620). Co-written with William Rowley.
Honourable Entertainments (1620–1)
An Invention (1622)
The Sun in Aries (1621)
The Triumphs of Honour and Virtue (1622)
The Triumphs of Integrity with The Triumphs of the Golden Fleece (1623)
The Triumphs of Health and Prosperity (1626)

Poetry

The Wisdom of Solomon Paraphrased (1597)
Microcynicon: Six Snarling Satires (1599)
The Ghost of Lucrece (1600)
Burbage epitaph (1619)
Bolles epitaph (1621)
Duchess of Malfi (commendatory poem) (1623)
St James (1623)
To the King (1624)

Prose

The Penniless Parliament of Threadbare Poets (1601)
News from Gravesend. Co-written with Thomas Dekker (1603)
The Nightingale and the Ant aka Father Hubbard's Tales (1604)
The Meeting of Gallants at an Ordinary (1604). Co-written with Thomas Dekker.
Plato's Cap Cast at the Year 1604 (1604)
The Black Book (1604)
Sir Robert Sherley his Entertainment in Cracovia (1609) (translation).
The Two Gates of Salvation (1609), or The Marriage of the Old and New Testament.
The Owl's Almanac (1618)
The Peacemaker (1618)

William Rowley – A Short Biography

William Rowley is thought to have been born around 1585 but an exact date is not known. As can be appreciated details of the lives of many people from centuries ago are hard to come by.

Rowley was an actor-playwright whose main early forte was playing 'clown characters' thus helping to carry the low comedy of the play.

The assumption is that he was a large man, since his speciality lay in fat-clown roles. He played the Fat Bishop in Thomas Middleton's A Game at Chess, and Plumporridge in the same author's Inner Temple Masque.

Rowley began his career working for Queen Anne's Men at the Red Bull Theatre. In 1609, he along with several other actors founded a new acting company, the Duke of York's Men, which, in 1612, became known as Prince Charles's Men.

From here on Rowley's career was spent almost exclusively writing and clowning for this company. It was located, in its time, at several playhouses, including the Curtain, the Hope, and the Red Bull.

Rowley was also the troupe's payee for their Court performances in the years 1610–15.

Scholars today are of the opinion that, as a writer, one of Rowley's main contributions in a play was to provide the comic sub-plot though on several plays, including The Changeling, A Fair Quarrel, and The Maid in the Mill, he wrote substantial portions of the main narrative as well.

Rowley also wrote fat-clown parts for himself to play: Jaques in All's Lost by Lust (a role "personated by the Poet," as it states in the 1633 quarto), and Bustopha in The Maid in the Mill, his collaboration with John Fletcher. He certainly played Simplicity in The World Tossed at Tennis, and most probably Chough in A Fair Quarrel both collaborations between himself and Thomas Middleton. As well, the part of the otherwise-unnamed Clown in The Birth of Merlin is again a role that Rowley the playwright wrote with Rowley the actor in mind.

As a writer, Rowley was almost exclusively a dramatist. The exception being a pamphlet; A Search for Money (1609). Only two surviving plays are generally accepted as solo works by Rowley: A Shoemaker, a Gentleman (circa 1607-9) and All's Lost by Lust (1619). Evidence exists that three other works were authored solely by Rowley: Hymen's Holidays or Cupid's Vagaries (1612), A Knave in Print (1613), and The Fool Without Book (also 1613) but unfortunately none have survived to be further examined.

In 1623, Rowley departed from his own company to join the very successful King's Men at the Globe, until his premature death in 1626. These final years though were certainly eventful. In 1624 he was embroiled in the Game at Chess controversy in August (this play was an allegory for the stormy relationship between Spain and Great Britain. Halted after only 9 performances it had already been hailed as a great hit. The Privy Council began a prosecution against the actors and the author of the play on 18th August as the law stated it was illegal to portray any modern Christian king on the stage. The Globe Theatre was shut down by the prosecution, though the author, Middleton, was able to acquit himself by showing that the play had been passed by the Master of the Revels, Sir Henry Herbert. However, the play was banned, and the actors reprimanded and fined. Middleton never wrote another play).

Four months later in December another crisis hit the King's Men when they performed The Spanish Viceroy (Relations between Britain and Spain were very tense at the time) without a licence from the Master of the Revels whose job was to oversee and censor all plays and collect the due fees. All the actors signed a written apology.

The roles he took with the King's Men are thought to have included Cacafogo in Rule a Wife and Have a Wife, the Cook in Rollo, Duke of Normandy, and Tony in A Wife for a Month.

He took a brief sojourn from the King's men in 1624 to work on the now lost play Keep the Widow Waking with Thomas Dekker, John Ford, and John Webster and which was to play at the Red Bull Theatre.

The exact time and nature of his death is unknown but records show that William Rowley was buried on 11th February 1626 in the graveyard of St James's, Clerkenwell in London

William Rowley – A Concise Bibliography

The works of William Rowley are difficult to confirm in many cases with absolute certainty. Rowley worked with many collaborators during his career. Complicating this is the fact that he was attributed as writer on several and on others that were his he received no credit.

All's Lost by Lust (performed 1618-19; printed 1633)

The Birth of Merlin; or, The Child Hath Found its Father (performed 1622; printed 1662). Originally published as co-authored by Shakespeare but this has little authority.

The Changeling (performed 1622; printed 1653) with Thomas Middleton.

A Cure for a Cuckold (performed 1624; printed 1661) with John Webster.

A Fair Quarrel (performed 1614-17; printed 1617) with Thomas Middleton.

Fortune by Land and Sea (performed c.1607; printed 1655) with Thomas Heywood.

The Maid in the Mill (performed 1623; printed 1647) with John Fletcher.

A Match at Midnight (performed c.1622; printed 1633). Attributed only to 'W. R.', and modern analysis suggests that it may not be by Rowley.

A New Wonder, a Woman Never Vexed (performed 1610-14; printed 1632). Possibly a collaboration; George Wilkins and Thomas Heywood have been suggested as co-writers.

The Old Law, or A New Way to Please You (performed 1618; printed 1656) with Thomas Middleton, and, possibly, a third collaborator who may have been Philip Massinger or Thomas Heywood.

A Shoemaker a Gentleman (date of composition unknown; printed 1638)

The Spanish Gypsy (performed 1623; printed 1653). Although the title page attributes this play to Rowley and Thomas Middleton, modern scholars are now leaning towards a playwriting team of John Ford and Thomas Dekker.

The Thracian Wonder (date of composition unknown; printed 1661) John Webster is also credited but modern scholars do now not accept this.

The Travels of the Three English Brothers (performed and printed 1607) written with George Wilkins and John Day.

Wit at Several Weapons (performed c.1615; printed 1647) Originally attributed to Beaumont and Fletcher modern scholars now believed the primary authors were by Rowley and Thomas Middleton.

The Witch of Edmonton (performed 1621; published 1658) written with John Ford and Thomas Dekker.

The World Tossed at Tennis (performed and printed 1620) written with Thomas Middleton.

www.ingramcontent.com/pod-product-compliance
Lightning Source LLC
Chambersburg PA
CBHW060116050426
42448CB00010B/1887